WELFARE-TO-WORK

Welfare-to-Work
New Labour and the US Experience

ANDREAS CEBULLA
National Centre for Social Research, UK

KARL ASHWORTH
Office for National Statistics, UK

DAVID GREENBERG
University of Maryland, Baltimore County, USA

ROBERT WALKER
University of Nottingham, UK

ASHGATE

Published by
Ashgate Publishing Limited
Gower House
Croft Road
Aldershot
Hants GU11 3HR
England

Ashgate Publishing Company
Suite 420
101 Cherry Street
Burlington, VT 05401-4405
USA

Ashgate website: http://www.ashgate.com

British Library Cataloguing in Publication Data
Welfare-to-Work : New Labour and the US experience
    1.Welfare recipients - Employment - Great Britain 2.Welfare
    recipients - Employment - United States 3.Insurance,
    Unemployment - Government policy - Great Britain
    4.Insurance, Unemployment - Government policy - United
    States 5.Unemployment - Government policy - Great Britain
    6.Unemployment - Government policy - United States
    I.Cebulla, Andreas
    362.5'8'0941

Library of Congress Cataloging-in-Publication Data
Welfare-to-work : New Labour and the US experience / by Andreas Cebulla ... [et al.].
    p. cm.
    Includes index.
    ISBN 0-7546-3775-1
    1. Welfare recipients--Employment--Great Britain. 2. Welfare recipients--
Employment--United States. 3. Public welfare--Great Britain. 4. Public welfare--
United States. 5. Great Britain--Politics and government--1979-1997. 6. Great
Britain--Politics and government--1997- 7. Evaluation research (Social action
programs)--United States. I. Cebulla, Andreas.

    HV248.W46 2004
    362.5'84'0941--dc22

                                                                    2004020998
ISBN 0 7546 3775 1

Printed and bound in Great Britain by MPG Books Ltd, Bodmin, Cornwall

Contents

List of Figures

List of Tables

List of Contributors

Andreas Cebulla is Research Director at the National Centre for Social Research, London. He was previously Assistant Director at the Centre for Research in Social Policy, Loughborough University.

Karl Ashworth is Principal Methodologist at the Office for National Statistics (ONS), Newport. Prior to joining ONS, he was Head of Statistical Resources at the Centre for Research in Social Policy, Loughborough University.

David Greenberg is Professor Emeritus at the Department of Economics, University of Maryland Baltimore County. Between 2000 and 2002, he was repeatedly Visiting Professor at the Centre for Research in Social Policy, Loughborough University.

Robert Walker is Professor of Social Policy, University of Nottingham. Until 1999, he was Professor of Social Policy and Director of the Centre for Research in Social Policy, Loughborough University.

Chapter 1

Welfare, Work and Welfare-to-Work in the UK

Andreas Cebulla and Robert Walker

Changing Welfare Policy in the UK

Welfare – defined to include social security and social assistance provision and its relationship to the labour market – and its reform have been recurrent themes in political and public debate in the United Kingdom since the early 1980s. After wholesale restructuring and 'salami-cutting' of provision under Conservative governments, welfare reform was at the heart of the electoral campaign of the rejuvenated *New* Labour Party elected to power in 1997. By championing a modernized political agenda, the Labour Party was able to shake off the public image of a party adhering to an outdated 'Old Left' ideology that had been a major obstacle to the party's re-election into government. In particular, plans to modernize welfare were used in support of Labour's claim that it could successfully manage the economy, a policy domain on which the Conservative Party had traditionally enjoyed a competitive advantage. The origins of these policies on welfare have fascinated political commentators and been the subject of largely inconclusive academic and journalistic study.

In 1979, when ousting the previous Labour Party government from power, the Conservative Party under Margaret Thatcher's leadership had famously claimed that 'Labour isn't working', depicting long and seemingly lengthening dole queues. By 1997, following a series of pre-election manifestos, the Labour Party had reversed the argument, highlighting what it saw as the Conservative government's failures to address inefficiencies in the public services, and, importantly, continued high levels of unemployment, especially among young people. It proposed a series of 'welfare-to-work' programmes that were later branded as 'the New Deals', designed to encourage welfare recipients to engage in a range of activities to help them prepare for and find work. By reducing claimant numbers, Labour hoped to release public funds for investment in education and health provision.

Although the reforms sometimes appear less radical in hindsight, they were notable for involving varying degrees of compulsion that meant that certain groups of recipients stood to lose benefit if they failed to co-operate, anathema to generations of Labour Party activists. While the shift from so-called 'passive' to 'active' welfare had been trailed by the Commission on Social Justice

(Commission on Social Justice, 1994), established when the Labour Party was briefly led by the late John Smith, it built on ideas, such as 'Project Work', that had been experimented with by the Conservatives, but previously ridiculed by the Labour opposition. The aim of this book is to understand the origins of Labour's pre-election u-turn on welfare reform and to assess the evidence, if any, upon which it was based.

The Conservative Years

In the years between 1979 and 1997, employment policies under the Conservative government underwent several transformations. Policies initially aimed at restructuring an economy that was losing markets and becoming internationally uncompetitive. The Conservatives' radical economic reforms included the calculated running-down of declining industries, most notably mining, the liberalization of trade relations, and the relaxation of restrictions on currency exchanges with a view to attracting international investment (Hutton, 1995; Middleton, 1999). In the process it both induced and reinforced a major cultural shift in society (Black, 2004). The demise of traditional, mainly manufacturing industries led to rising unemployment, but new service sector jobs emerged, albeit slowly and typically not in areas that had suffered industrial decline. In the period between 1983 and 1986 both employment and unemployment, in particular long-term unemployment, increased, although in different locations across the country, sharpening the North-South economic divide.

In the early years of the Conservative government, industrial policy, previously the Labour government's favourite policy instrument, was replaced by an emphasis on monetary policy as the main principle of economic policy making. The aim was tightly to control the circulation of money in the economy in an attempt to reign in inflation and to keep it low so as to encourage private sector investment. In the mid-1980s, the economy was given a further boost as reductions in corporate and personal taxes unleashed, as intended, new consumer spending and commercial, often speculative, investment (the 'Lawson Boom'). Shortly afterwards, the Government's monetary policy changed with the decision to shadow the German Mark and to enter the European Exchange Rate Mechanism (ERM). While, on the one hand, new consumer and investor spending contributed to rising inflation, the Government's efforts to tie the British economy in with that of Europe produced pressures to curtail inflation. As interest rates rose, so did personal debt. The Lawson Boom fizzled out and unemployment, which had temporarily stabilized, began to rise again.

Both the unemployment crisis of the early 1980s and of the early 1990s triggered fresh concerns about how the number of (long-term) unemployed benefit claimants could be reduced. Early thinking tended to be guided as much by ideology as by learning from policy and experience. There was little understanding of the workings of the labour market under unprecedented high levels of unemployment and only rudimentary appreciation of the social consequences of unemployment, the scale of which had last been experienced in the 1930s. The American author Charles Murray emerged as a key figure that would influence and perpetuate conservative thinking about the – allegedly – voluntary nature of long-term unemployment, induced by seemingly generous social security provisions. Murray was given the opportunity by the Sunday Times newspaper on a number of occasions to repeat his ideas of the adverse effects of the receipt of social security benefits, which he had already propagated to great acclaim in the US (Murray, 1989; Man and Roseneil, 1994). His warning of the 'emergence of a British Underclass' received much attention as politicians, policymakers and the public became increasingly concerned about unrelentingly high numbers of benefit claimants in the UK (Walker with Howard, 2000). If they were not already, Murray's claims also ensured that British policy makers and analysts became keen observers of US welfare reform policies. From the mid-1980s, beginning with the Restart interviews (see Chapter 7), an increasing number of initiatives or reform pilots designed to reduce the number of benefit claimants were introduced informed by initiatives first tried in the US.

This phase of piecemeal experimentation with welfare reform measures designed to 'activate' the unemployed into jobseeking intensified in the 1990s, as unemployment remained high and more news about innovative and apparently successful endeavours in active labour market policy emerged, principally from the US. Whereas most of these early initiatives in the UK were subject to post-hoc evaluation, public scrutiny of the efficacy of policy innovation climaxed considerably later, coinciding with – and perhaps influenced by – New Labour's electoral claim and promise that, if in government, it would base its policy on the collection and use of *evidence*: 'evidence-based policy-making'.

Labour and the New Deal

The New Deal was one of the flagship policies of New Labour's 1997 election campaign. Beside increased investment in education and the National Health Service, the party vociferously advocated a new programme to eradicate unemployment, in particular among young people, and help benefit claimants in their transition from welfare to work. This programme was more than just a policy. A new language of policymaking and promotion emerged, which argued that modern politics needed to be based on a new contract between the state as provider of services and facilitator of opportunities and the individual citizen as the user and beneficiary of these services and opportunities (Giddens, 1998, 2000, 2003). In other words, New Labour offered the nation a deal, a new deal, which later became the New Deal.

The notion of a contract between the state and her citizens was not simply conceptual. Legislation introduced by the Conservative government in 1996 to replace Unemployment Benefit by Jobseeker's Allowance (JSA) already required benefit claimants to sign a Jobseeker's Agreement, which detailed, amongst other things, what the claimant was expected to do in terms of job search and improving his or her chances of finding paid work. Under New Labour, certain categories of claimants were also obliged under contract to participate in a range of training and work experience options. Furthermore, over time, the number and range of claimants compelled to engage with work-related activities has continued to expand. In the process a new kind of social security official has been created, the personal adviser, whose job entails monitoring and liasing with claimants to speed their return to paid employment.

Eight New Deal programmes are currently in place,[1] although not all of them receive the same level of public and policy attention (Table 1). In two of these, the New Deal for Young People and the New Deal for 25 plus, participation is compulsory and for a third, New Deal for Lone Parents, attendance at an interview with a Personal Advisor is mandatory, although their subsequent participation in the job training and placement programme is voluntary. In all other instances, participation is voluntary, although work-focused interviews are gradually being made mandatory for all claimants of working age with the national roll-out of Jobcentre Plus offices.

In terms of annual expenditure, the New Deal for Young People remains, by far, the largest programme. The only other programme attracting significant amounts of programme expenditure as a result of the large number of participants is the New Deal for 25 plus. Programme expenditure includes allowances paid to programme participants, who do not receive a wage, and employer subsidies. Administrative expenditure tends to be lower than programme costs, with the exception of the New Deal for Lone Parents (NDLP) programme, which is primarily an advice based service.

True to its word, the Labour government implemented a programme of evaluation studies designed to monitor and assess the effectiveness of the New Deal programmes and their individually tailored contents, many conducted as pilots prior to full national implementation of policies. Most of these studies were commissioned by one of the two government departments that, prior to 2002, were responsible for education and employment policies, and for social security: the Department for Work and Pensions (previously the Department of Social Security) and the Department for Employment and Skills (previously the Department for Education and Employment). Policy debates have since focussed on reviewing the evidence that has been collected from the array of evaluation studies (DWP, 2004; Willetts, 2002).

Beyond the applied policy debates, academic research has sought to identify the ideological roots and to track the ultimate source of New Labour's programme ideas, which represented a clear departure from traditional (or 'Old') Labour policies. To prepare their respective case, contributors to this debate have drawn on selective reviews of apparent parallels in welfare-to-work programmes, mostly in the US, but also in Australia and, to a much lesser extent, in New Zealand and the Netherlands. This book contributes to the debate in two ways. First, it explores the nature and origin of the New Deal in the UK, how New Labour developed and civil servants implemented a fine-tuned welfare-to-work programme. Secondly, it provides a comprehensive assessment of the

---

[1] A ninth programme, the New Deal for Communities, is an area-based initiative, which aims to address various aspects of concentrated social and economic disadvantage experienced in some neighbourhoods, such as residents' poor health conditions, as well as high levels of unemployment.

Table 1.1   New Deal Programmes in the United Kingdom

New Deal for	Target group	Compulsion	Programme Expenditure[1] (2001/02; £m)	Administrative Expenditure[1] (2001/02/ £m)
Young People (NDYP)	18- to 24-year olds who have been unemployed and claiming Jobseeker's Allowance for 6 months or more	Yes	219	89
25 plus (ND25 plus)	Individuals aged 25 or over who have been claiming Jobseeker's Allowance for 18 months or more	Yes	140	73
50plus	Individuals 50 or over in receipt of Income Support, Jobseeker's Allowance, Incapacity Benefit or Severe Disablement Allowance for six months or more	No	2	5
Disabled people	Recipients of a range of incapacity- or disability-related social security benefits	No	4	6
Lone parents	Lone parents who work less than 16 hours per week or not at all and with children below the age of 16	Yes[2]	9	37
Partners	Partners of recipients of Income Support, Jobseeker's Allowance, Incapacity Benefit, Carer's Allowance or Severe Disablement Allowance	No	2	6
Self-employment	All New Deal participants who wish to try self-employment	No	N/a[3]	N/a[3]
Musicians	Participants in NDYP or ND25 plus who wish to develop a career in the music industry	No	N/a[3]	N/a[3]

[1] DWP (2003).
[2] First interview with Personal Advisor only.
[3] Included in the other New Deal programmes, through which participants had originally entered the programme.

deliberations of civil servants and politicians before, during and after the establishing of the New Deal in the UK.

Welfare Reform in the US

US welfare-to-work policy can be traced back to the 1981 Omnibus Budget Reconciliation Act (OBRA), which was adopted by Congress shortly after the inauguration of Ronald Reagan as US President. OBRA allowed US states to require recipients of social assistance, Aid to Families with Dependent Children (AFDC), to participate in mandatory job search or job training activities, or to join the Community Work Experience Program, which made participants work for benefits. In many cases, these policies could not be implemented state-wide for logistical and budget reasons even though Federal law required AFDC programmes to be available on the same terms to all state residents. However, federal law also included provisions for granting exceptions – waivers – for investigating the consequences of changing programme rules in ways judged by the Department of Health, Education, and Welfare (now the Department of Health and Human Services) to further the ends of the law. States took the opportunity of waivers to introduce a range of policy developments including modification of the financial incentives offered to make paid work more attractive, sanctions for non-compliance where programmes were mandatory, and new and/or more intensive provision of support services to participants when compared to the AFDC programme. Typically, traditional AFDC programmes continued to be run alongside the new experimental programmes.

Policies implemented under waivers were generally required to be evaluated and such evaluation often took the form of policy experiments with potential participants being randomly assigned either to a programme group exposed to the policy or to a control group that was denied access to it. This requirement resulted in a wealth of evaluation studies being produced, which ultimately made the present study possible. It also led to the expansion of a policy evaluation industry in the US, which began to set new and higher standards of evaluation not only in the US, but also beyond. In 1986, the first evaluation of a welfare reform programme triggered by OBRA was published by MDRC (Friedlander, et al., 1986). Most US evaluations conducted since have been undertaken by MDRC, the US market leader in the evaluation of welfare reform programmes, Abt Associates Inc. and Mathematica, although numerous independent and University-based research teams have also contributed in various ways to the burgeoning US evaluation industry.

Until 1988, AFDC was generally only available to lone parent families and hence the OBRA legislation was solely concerned with 'activating' one-parent families. Their rising numbers had been the main focus of concern among US politicians, policymakers and media (Gans, 1995). It was also to lone parents that Charles Murray initially applied the label 'underclass' – a phrase originally coined by the Swedish economist Gunnar Myrdal in the 1960s (Myrdal, 1963) to describe, non-pejoratively, a population at risk of social and economic exclusion.

In 1988, the Family Support Act (FSA) widened the target population of welfare-to-work programmes to include two-parent families and introduced a new federal training, education, placement services and community work experience programme, the Job Opportunities and Basic Skills (JOBS). It not only mandated states to use random assignment methodology in conducting evaluations under waiver programmes, it also required States to prepare 'employability plans' for participants of their programmes. It thus introduced the concept of case management, which has since become a key component of labour market activation programmes in the US and beyond.

Under President Bill Clinton, who entered office in 1993, welfare waivers were granted more liberally and more frequently than at any time before (Wiseman, 2002) as Clinton pursued his pre-election pledge to 'end welfare as we know it' (Weaver, 2000). In 1996, the Clinton administration passed the Personal Responsibility and Work Opportunity Reconciliation Act (PRWORA), which removed the states' obligation to seek approval for reform programmes and allowed them to set their own welfare eligibility criteria. Most significantly, however, PRWORA introduced a five-year lifetime limit on the receipt of social assistance, now renamed Temporary Assistance for Needy Families (TANF), and a two-year limit for continuous welfare receipt, although exemptions for up to 20 per cent of a State's caseload are permissible.

TANF was initially given a five-year life and was required to be re-enacted by Congress in 2002. At the time of writing (June 2004), TANF was still awaiting this re-enactment, better known as re-authorization. The delay has been due to disagreement between Democrat and Republican representatives in the US Senate over the extent to which conditions under TANF should be further tightened. In the meantime, Congress has been granting short-term extension of current TANF provision, typically running for three months.

The Challenge of Evidence-Based Policy-Making

Soon after its election into government in 1997, Labour declared that evidence-based policy-making was to be at the heart of its policy formulation. New policy initiatives were to be vigorously evaluated to learn about their strengths and weaknesses, their effectiveness, and to ensure that modifications were undertaken where programmes performed sub-optimally. This emphasis on evidence to inform policy making was, of course, not entirely new. Previous governments had also evaluated their policies, although only recent developments in research methodology strengthened the position of evaluation and of the evaluator in informing policy. However, the Labour government not only promoted more research and, sometimes innovative, evaluation of its policies. It also set up new structures that would promote policy evaluation and the reflection upon evaluation findings' implications for policy practice, albeit, it may be argued, within the boundaries of prevailing political agendas.

The prime role of policy co-ordinator across ministerial departments within government was assigned to the Cabinet Office, which was charged with ensuring that Government delivers on its key priorities, 'aiming at excellence in policy making and responsive, high quality public services' (Cabinet Office website, 11 June 2004). Following the 1999 publication of the White Paper 'Modernising Government' (Cm., 1999), it produced a series of manuals for policy makers including 'Professional policy making in the 21st Century' (Cabinet Office, 1999), 'Adding it up' (Cabinet Office, 2000) and 'Better Policy Making' (Cabinet Office, 2001) that emphasized the enhanced role that should be accorded to evidence. It also pioneered the now discontinued People Panels. The Panels consisted of about 5000 randomly selected members of the public, who, between 1998 and January 2002, were consulted on topics of public policy interest, including such diverse subjects as school performance tables, the standard of public services, and research in human genetics. The Panels were abolished after three years when the decision was taken to de-centralize responsibility for improving public services from the Cabinet Office to the government departments and agencies (People Panels, special announcement, March 2002).

More recently, strategic oversight of evidence-based policy-making, now often restated as 'evidence-informed' has shifted to the Prime Minister's Strategy Unit (SU) which has become the main principal charged with '... providing the Prime Minister and Government departments with a capacity to analyse major policy issues and design strategic solutions...' (Strategy Unit website at www.number10.gov.uk/output/Page77.asp). This resulted from an amalgamation, in 2002, of the Prime Minister's Forward Strategy Unit (FSU) with the Performance and Innovation Unit (PIU), based in the Cabinet Office, and parts of the Centre for Management and Policy Studies (CMPS), a separate division within the Cabinet Office. All three organizations had previously performed similar and related *strategic* policy tasks, which were pooled under the auspices of the Unit as a result of the amalgamation. Since then, the Strategy Unit has published 'forward-thinking reports' in such diverse range fields as risk management (Strategy Unit, 2002a), electronic networks (Strategy Unit, 2002b) and the status of ethnic minorities in the British labour market (Strategy Unit, 2003).

Within the Strategy Unit, the key role of promoting standards of research and evaluation methodology within government and in conducting innovative evaluation projects has fallen to the Government Chief Social Researcher's Office (GCSRO). Its tasks also include the co-ordination of research between government department, improving the accessibility of past and current research and research findings within government, and ensuring that government researchers have the necessary skills and competences for conducting and monitoring (commissioned) high-quality social research. It also maintains and publishes the so-called 'Magenta Book' of guidance on policy evaluation (GCSCO, 2004) that complements HM Treasury's 'Green Book' concerned with economic appraisal.

There are 1,000 civil servants in 19 government departments belonging to the Government Social Research service (GSR) who often work closely with government economists and statisticians and are increasingly located in policy divisions to try to ensure the connection between research and policymaking.

Exact figures of socio-economic research spending are not readily available, but a recent review established that *all* research and development spending rose from £1.28bn in 1998/9 to £1.57bn in 2001/02 and in 2002/03 (HMT, 2002). In its Spending Review of 2002, the government promised that these figures be further increased over the next few years. Much of this research spending, however, was and will continue to be concentrated in science and technology rather than social research. It will also be conducted in and on behalf of government departments rather than the GCSRO, which conducts or commissions little research itself. Nevertheless, the GCSRO epitomizes the Labour government's quest for evidence-based policy-making, gathering and distributing national and international information and guidance notes designed to inform and improve policy evaluation.

Critiques of Evidence-Based Policy-making

The concept of evidence-based policy-making is, however, not without its critics who argue that evidence-based policy-making (EBPM) is much more constrained by *methodological uncertainty* than its empiricist approach and undercurrent of positivism suggests (Hammersley, 2002; Marks, 2002). Research findings, it has been argued, are far less precise and much more uncertain than proponents of EBPM appears to concede (Hammersley, 2001). Furthermore, the impact of EBPM on policy may be much less than advocates of EBPM would like to think or will ever be able to achieve. After all, *policy-making* is the outcome of many complementary and conflicting processes and influences, of which evidence is only one (as illustrated in Levitt, 2003). Evidence does not immediately translate into practice, but is subject to political negotiations and haggling for positions of power (Perri 6, 2002).

From a methodological point of view, however, the main point of contention is EBPM's approach to assessing, rating and ranking evidence. This criticism is particularly directed at systematic reviews, which, in principle if less often in practice, form a key element in EBPM (Boaz et al., 2002). EBPM requires evidence to be rated and ranked in order identify robust and reliable studies and de-select or place less weight on those less or not at all reliable. Such decisions to rate and rank studies it typically built on their methodological rigour. Critics have, however, argued that the process of assessment is fraught with subjective judgments, which render assessments highly contestable and more so than proponents of systematic reviews tend to admit (Hammersley, 2002). Even slight adjustments to the differential weighting that is applied to evaluations in systematic reviews may thus suddenly change a review's findings.

The principal advocates of, and the archives for, systematic reviews are the Cochrane Collaboration, which deals primarily with research in medicine and health, and the rapidly expanding, but more recent Campbell Collaboration, which is concerned with social, educational, psychological and criminological research evidence. Both organizations – the Campbell Collaboration largely following the lead of the Cochrane Collaboration – stress in their guidance materials the need to select and rank research and evaluation studies prior to their inclusion in systematic reviews. This prioritization process builds on a hierarchy of preferred research methods, at the top of which are randomized controlled trials (RCT), because 'randomization is the only means of allocation that controls for unknown and unmeasured confounders as well as for those known and measured' (Andersen et al., 2004, p. 54).

The Cochrane Collaboration is much more cautious with respect to non-experimental studies, arguing

> the nature of observational studies makes them even more difficult to critically appraise [than RCT, the authors]. This requires a thorough understanding of both the problem that is the focus of the review and methodological considerations. Caution is needed (Anderson et al., 2004, p. 56).

The Non-randomized Studies Methods Group of the Cochrane Collaboration is currently preparing guidelines for assessing non-experimental, observational studies. In the meantime, the lack of adequate guidance of how to treat non-randomized, observational data in systematic reviews and the strong reputation of RCT might, authors like Hammersley fear, lead to the exclusion of, on its own, perfectly adequate and robust evidence on suspicious grounds of technical inferiority. Thus, systematic reviews might themselves become biased.

More recently, EBPM has been the subject of critique by proponents of 'realistic evaluation' (Pawson and Tilley, 1997), who have positioned themselves as one of the main challengers of the empiricism of systematic review (Nutley, 2003). Their main concern is not only that evaluation studies – in systematic reviews or more generally – are of good quality, but that their quality should not be assessed according to some 'objective' and allegedly universal criterion. Rather assessments ought to take explicit account of the specificity of the research issues that evaluations address and of the social context, within which studies are set (Pawson, n.d.).

Pawson is critical of systematic review and its statistical tool, meta-analysis, because of what he perceives to be the method's propensity to identify 'sub-types of programmes' (Pawson, 2002, p. 341), which are found to work well within a range of programmes, and to suggest they be reassembled to form a new entity of programme altogether: 'Knowledge transfer is a matter of identifying and imitating the most powerful classes of programmes (or eliminating the most dangerous).' (ibid.) This approach, he argues, ignores the situational context, in which programmes succeed or fail.

While Pawson's valid criticism is well taken, it is also one that meta-analysis ought to be able to address. Systematic reviews and meta-analysis need not be operating context-free, nor do they pretend to be – any more than other research methods. The challenge that systematic review and meta-analysis face is to 'operationalize' the multi-layered and multi-faceted context in the same way as narrative and realist reviews do or seek to do. No method is ever likely to account for 'context' in its entirety. The least that systematic reviews and meta-analysis can do is to make a start and explore the extent to which further contextual information might be needed to account better for the changes, and variations in changes, that evaluations observe.

Meta-Analysis

A large part of this book reports the method and results of a meta-analysis of US welfare-to-work programmes. Perhaps in a manner, which oversimplifies the complexity of the endeavour, meta-analysis has been defined as a 'method of averaging results across studies' (Hunter and Schmidt, 1990, p.13). Lipsey and Wilson (2000) are a little more precise in their definition of meta-analysis, which, they say, 'extracts detailed and differentiated information about the quantitative findings of each study [included in the meta-analysis, the authors] and incorporates it in a database along with coded information about important features of the source study' (ibid., p. 1).

Although Lispey's and Wilson's definition presents an advance over Hunter's and Schmidt's in so far as it acknowledges the importance of adding 'coded information about important features of the source study', it is still insufficient to address Pawson's concerns about the narrow focus of meta-analysis. It is clearly essential to incorporate data about the features of studies into the database and, ultimately, the structure of the meta-analysis. These data determine the weight given to individual studies in the analysis on the basis of their statistical precision (see Chapter 4). However, in addition to paying attention to the 'statistical inequities' among evaluation studies, meta-analysis will need to acknowledge that the social and economic context, in which programmes assessed in the analysis operate, inevitably vary. To control for this variability, further 'control variables' need to be introduced.

The US welfare-to-work evaluations included in the meta-analysis in this book are limited to those that used random assignment techniques. Random allocation of eligible individuals to the programme group or to the control group without access to the programme works on the assumption that differences in the experiences that are being monitored between the two groups will be due to the programme or participation in the programme. Randomization, in effect, controls for other known and unknown, measured and unmeasured or un-measurable influences. However, this is only true for the individual study. Aggregated in systematic reviews and meta-analysis, evaluations describe events that took place at different times and in different locations. While both are likely to effect programme outcomes, neither is the result of random allocation. The 'internal randomization' of evaluations is not matched by their 'external randomization' as they enter the meta-analysis database. In its absence, control variables are required to approximate contextual differences between programmes and their evaluations.

The two key indicators of difference that will be reported in this book are programme participants' and non-participants' earnings and the proportion of participants and non-participants continuing to receive social assistance payments, in this instance, Aid to Families with Dependent Children (AFDC). The objective is to estimate the *impacts* of programmes, that is, the net difference between the earnings or prevalence of AFDC receipt among programme participants and non-participants over time. In doing so, further variables will be added to the database and the analysis in order to control for differences in the characteristics and, with respect to job search and training, activities of programme participants and non-participants. Moreover, and rarely for meta-analysis, variations in the characteristics of programme locations will be taken into account. This will allow a more differentiated and critically reflective assessment of the impacts and the effectiveness of welfare-to-work programmes in the US than meta-analytic methods have usually achieved.

The analyses reported here, therefore, are set within a wider analytical frame. By controlling for contextual features, in which each individual welfare-to-work programme was set and which, most likely, affected their outcomes, the current approach goes beyond the averaging of study results associated with conventional meta-analysis. It may be more appropriately described as *meta-evaluation* – an evaluation of evaluations, which takes explicit account of the type of intervention originally evaluated and of social and economic context in which it is located.

Structure of the Book

This book is divided into eight chapters. In the next chapter (Chapter 2), Andreas Cebulla provides a detailed account of the evolution of the New Deal welfare-to-work programme in the UK. As already noted, the New Deal programme was introduced by the incoming Labour government in early 1997 and has since been the cornerstone of active labour market policy in Britain. While primarily, albeit not exclusively, targeted at claimants of out-of-work social security benefits (Jobseeker's Allowance, Income Support), the programme, which has been subjected to repeated and often longitudinal evaluation studies, has become the proto-type for derivative and more specialist welfare-to-work programmes aimed at groups of benefit claimants that the New Deal has tended not to reach. The New Deal has, thus, become a model for developing and expanding welfare-to-work programmes within the UK, and the approach has attracted interest internationally. In his chapter, Cebulla draws on interviews with UK politicians, policy makers and policy analysts to re-trace the origins of the New Deal concept and the nature of its implementation. He highlights the importance of both, US American and Scandinavian influences, transmitted via direct and indirect contacts, and also the roles and interest of the two key government departments involved in the programme's implementation: the Department of Social Security and the Department for Education and Employment.

In Chapter 3, Cebulla extends his analysis of the UK New Deal, to focus more closely on the process of implementation and the balance between (external) policy transfer (from the US or Sweden) and (internal) institutional learning. His analysis emphasizes the importance of path dependency and hence the need to understand the evolution of New Deal from the much more piecemeal welfare-to-work programmes in the UK prior to 1997. He also explores the contribution of evaluation evidence to the implementation process.

Contributions to this book then turn to reviewing the evaluation evidence of welfare-to-work programmes in the United States. First, in Chapter 4, Greenberg and Ashworth describe the statistical method of meta-analysis that was used to analyse evaluations of 64 US welfare-to-work programmes. The authors provide background information about the type of evaluation studies included in the meta-analysis and the rationale for their selection. The principal findings and key issues arising from previous US welfare-to-work evaluations, including comparative studies, are summarized. The analysis is situated within the broader context of the development of welfare-to-work programmes in the US.

In Chapter 5, Ashworth and Greenberg present descriptive results of their meta-analysis of US welfare-to-work programmes, thus providing illustrations of the programmes' variability in content and effectiveness. The authors focus, in particular, on the characteristics of welfare-to-work programmes, highlighting programmes, which have emphasized training over work-placements and vice versa. They also pay specific attention to the characteristics of programme participants and the economic conditions prevailing in the programme areas at the time of their evaluation, as these features critically influenced the programmes' impacts.

Greenberg and Walker pick up the theme again in Chapter 6, describing and discussing the findings of the meta-analysis of US welfare-to-work programmes. Going beyond the descriptive results of the previous chapter, the authors examine why some welfare-to-work programmes performed better than others, demonstrating how meta-analysis was able to highlight important differences between programmes, which affected their performance. The analysis focuses, in particular, on the impact of programmes on average earnings and on the proportion of programme participants who received social assistance (Aid to Families with Dependent Children). In a separate analysis, the authors explore the extent to which the fact that some programmes outperformed others was the result of advantageous programme features or reflected differences in the characteristics of participants or economic factors, which worked in some programmes' favour, but disadvantaged others.

In Chapter 7, Cebulla takes a broader look at the evolution of active labour market policy in the UK, in particular the turn away from training programmes and towards programmes, which aimed to place the unemployed immediately into paid employment. Cebulla summarizes the evaluation evidence of the UK's most prominent labour market policies of the (late) 1980s and 1990s, and presents the findings from comparative studies of the effectiveness of training programmes in the US. He finally turns to the debate concerning the contribution of welfare-to-work programmes to the observed reduction in the national and regional welfare caseloads in the US relative to the influence that wider macro-economic improvements might have had, which occurred at the same time.

Finally, Chapter 8 draws together the key findings of the analyses presented in this book and examines the policy implications of the research findings for the UK New Deal, the potential for meta-analysis to inform social policymaking, and the conditions that would enhance the scope for meta-analysis and systematic review in policy development. In particular, the authors, Greenberg and Cebulla, address the questions of whether UK policy has learned the 'right' lessons from the US experience and what other lessons might be learned. A critical finding from Chapter 6 was that specific elements of welfare-to-work programmes, socio-economic conditions and the characteristics of programme participants had all made their mark on the impacts of welfare-to-work programmes in the US. Against this background, Greenberg and Cebulla ask whether programme administrators could, in fact, 'design' programmes for greater effectiveness, taking account of the critical factors identified in the meta-analysis.

References

Anderson, P., Green, S. and Higgins, J.P.T. (eds.) (2004), *Cochrane Reviewers' Handbook 4.2.2.* Updated March 2004.
www.cochrane.org\resources\handbook\hbook.htm (accessed 23 April 2004).

Black, J. (2004), *Britain since the seventies – politics and society in the consumer age,* Reaktion Books, London.

Boaz, A., Ashby, D. and Young, K. (2002), *Systematic Reviews: what have they got to offer evidence-based policy and practice,* ESRC UK Centre for Evidence Based Policy and Practice Working Paper No. 2, University of London, London.

Cabinet Office (1999), *Professional Policy Making in the 21st Century,* Cabinet Office, London.

Cabinet Office (2000), *Adding it up*, Cabinet Office, London.

Cabinet Office (2001), *Better Policy Making*, Cabinet Office, London.

Commission on Social Justice (1994), *Social Justice: Strategies for National Renewal*, Institute for Public Policy Research, London.

Cm. (1999), *Modernising Government* (White Paper), Cm 4310, London.

DWP (2003), *Department Report 2003*, Department for Work and Pensions, London.

DWP (2004), *Building on New Deal: Local solutions meeting individual needs*, Department for Work and Pensions, London.

Friedlander, D., et al, (1986) *West Virginia: Final Report on the Community Work Experience Demonstrations*, MDRC, New York.

Gans, H.J. (1995), *The war against the poor – the underclass and antipoverty policy*, Basic Books, New York.

Giddens, A. (1998), *The Third Way*, Polity Press, Cambridge.

Giddens, A. (2000), *The Third Way and Its Critics*, Polity Press, Cambridge.

Giddens, A. (2003), 'The third way: the renewal of social democracy ' in A. Chadwick and R. Heffernan (eds.) *The New Labour Reader*, Polity Press, Cambridge.

Hales, J. et al. (2000), *Evaluation of the New Deal for Lone Parents: early Lessons from the Phase One Prototype – Synthesis Report*, Department for Work and Pensions Research Report 108, Corporate Document Services, Leeds.

Hammersley, M. (2001), *Some questions about evidence-based practice in education.* Paper presented at the symposium on 'Evidence-based practice in education' at the Annual Conference of the British

Educational Research Association, University of Leeds, England, September 13-15, 2001.

Hammersley, M. (2002a), *Educational Research, Policymaking, and Practice*, Paul Chapman, London.

Hammersley, M. (2002b), *Systematic or unsystematic – is that the question? Some reflections on the science, art, and politics of reviewing research evidence*. Talk to the Public Health Evidence Steering Group of the Health Development Agency, October.

HMT (2002), *Cross-cutting review of science and research: final report*, HM Treasury, London.

Hunter, J.E. and Schmidt, F.L. (1990), *Methods of Meta-Analysis – Correcting error and bias in research findings*, Sage, London.

Hutton, W. (1995), *The State We're in. Why Britain is in crisis and how to overcome it*, Vintage Books, London.

Levitt, R. (2003), *GM crops and food. Evidence, policy and practise in the UK: a case study*. ESRC UK Centre for Evidence Based Policy and Practise Working Paper No. 20, University of London, London.

Lipsey, M.W. and Wilson, D.B. (2000), *Practical Meta-Analysis*, Sage: New York.

Mann, K. and Roseneil, S. (1994), 'Some mothers do 'ave 'em': backlash and the gender politics of the underclass debate', *Journal of Gender Studies*, vol. 3.3, pp. 317-331.

Marks, D.F. (2002), *Perspectives on evidence-based practice*. Health Development Agency, London.

Middleton, R. (1999), *The British economy since 1945*. Palgrave Macmillan, Basingstoke.

Murray, C. (1989), *Underclass*, Sunday Times Magazine, November 26, 1989.

Myrdal, G. (1963), *Challenge of Affluence*, Pantheon, New York.

Nutley, S. (2003), *Bridging the policy/research divide. Reflections and lessons from the UK*. Keynote paper presented at the 'Facing the future: engaging stakeholders and citizens in developing public policy' conference of the National Institute of Governance, Canberra, Australia, 23/24 April.

Pawson, R. (n.d.), *Assessing the quality of evidence in evidence-based policy: why, how and when?* ESRC Research Methods Programme, Working Paper No.1. http://www.ccsr.ac.uk/methods/publications.

Pawson, R. (2002), 'Evidence-based Policy: The promise of 'realist synthesis'', *Evaluation*, vol. 3, pp. 340-358.

Pawson, R. and Tilley, N. (1997), *Realistic Evaluation*, Sage, London.

People Panels (2002), *Special Announcement*, March, www.cabinet-office.gov.uk/servicefirst/2001/panel/newsletter.final.htm

Perri 6 (2002), 'Can policy-making be evidence-based?', *Managing community care*, Vol. 10.1, pp. 3-8.

Strategy Unit (2002a), *Risk: improving government's capability to handle risk and uncertainty*, Cabinet Office, London.

Strategy Unit (2002b), *Electronic Networks – Challenges for the Next Decade*, Cabinet Office, London.

Strategy Unit (2003), *Ethnic Minorities and the Labour Market – Final Report*, Cabinet Office, London.

Walker, R. (2000), 'Learning if policy will work: The case of New Deal for Disabled People', *Policy Studies*, Vol. 21.4, pp. 313-345.

Walker, R., (2001), 'Great Expectations: Can social science evaluate New Labour's policies?', *Evaluation,* Vol. 7.3, pp. 305-330.

Walker, R., with Howard, M. (2000), *The Making of a Welfare Class? Benefit Receipt in Britain*, Policy Press, Bristol.

Weaver, R.K. (2000), *Ending welfare as we know it*, Brookings Institution Press, Washington.

Willetts, D (2002), *Labour's Failed Welfare-to-Work Schemes: Time for a crackdown on crackdowns.* 25 November, www.davidwilletts.org.uk/record.jsp?type=article&ID=15&sectionID =2, visited 22 June 2004.

Wiseman, M. (2003), 'Welfare in the United States', in R. Walker and M. Wiseman (eds.), *The welfare we want?   The British challenge for American reform*, The Policy Press, Bristol.

Chapter 2

The Road to Britain's 'New Deal'

Andreas Cebulla

Introduction

> The truth is that there has been just as much influence on New Labour's policies from Europe as from the US. What we are doing on welfare to work and jobs is closely in line with the policies that have been developed over many years in the Netherlands, Denmark and Sweden (Mulgan, 1998, p. 19).

On its arrival in government in the spring of 1997, *New* Labour introduced a set of active labour market and welfare policy reforms. Following repeated election defeats in the 1980s and 1990s, New Labour had changed its political agenda, culminating in the adoption of a new party ideology and a new approach to policy making, which also affected its stance on welfare policy. The party scaled down the interventionist and demand-side orientated economic and social policies, such as openly progressive taxation, anti-cyclical capital spending and maintaining nationalized industries that had featured in its manifestos in the 1970s and 1980s. Whereas the Labour Party of the 1970s expressed belief in promoting prosperity and social solidarity – today's expression 'social cohesion' was not used then – through economic management, New Labour has a narrower perception of the role of the state and the scope for effective government intervention. The notion that solidarity can be promoted and engineered by state institutions has been replaced by concepts of individual rights and responsibilities, which emphasize citizen's obligation to contribute to their own and the collective well-being.

The New Deal reflects this transformation in political thinking, combining the right to state services and universal coverage with the responsibility of target populations to participate in the support schemes that the programme offers. This emphasis on responsibility is clearest for the target populations of young people and long-term unemployed, for whom participation in the New Deal programmes is compulsory, while for other groups (lone parents, the over-50s) participation is voluntary, but actively encouraged. In fact, recent changes to the New Deal for Lone Parents have made participation in introductory *work-focused interviews* with Jobcentre case workers compulsory, although the decision whether to participate subsequently in the support programme proper is still the lone parent's. The gradual national roll-out of *Jobcentre Plus*, integrating (and ultimately replacing) Jobcentres, which provide jobseekers with employment advice and placements, and the Benefit Agency, which administers social security benefits, will progressively extend the use of case workers in the administration of benefits. This transition is set to lead – and, in fact, is already leading – to the increased use of mandatory work-focussed interviews in both active benefits, where claimants are expected to *actively seek work*, and inactive benefits, where they are not.

In the course of conceptualising the New Deal, New Labour took inspiration from diverse sources. The apparent parallels between the New Deal and US welfare-to-work programmes, in particular their ideological affinity, have received considerable attention amongst students of policy transfer (Deacon, 2000; Peck and Theodore, 2001; Walker, 1999). Several authors have also emphasized other external influences, above all Australian (Finn, 1998, 1999; Johnson and Tonkiss, 2002). Scandinavian influences have also been acknowledged (Mulgan, 1998).

In this chapter, the influence of the US welfare-to-work experience and of other theoretical and practical welfare models on New Labour's design of the New Deal is scrutinized within the context of the party's search for a new identity. Peck and Theodore (2001, p. 449) have argued that the manifestation and nature of the New Deal can only be understood in the context of 'prevailing political-economic conditions within the UK, the roots of which can be traced to the "modernization" of the Labour Party under [Prime Minister] Blair's leadership'. The analysis takes this claim as a starting point to explore how party policy and economic and welfare concepts have shaped the New Deal. It integrates evidence from secondary sources with that of interviews conducted with policy makers and policy analysts in the Departments of Social Security (now Department for Work and Pensions) and for Education and Employment (now Department for Education and Skills) and Her Majesty's Treasury. Members of Parliament and the House of Lords, and researchers in academe and policy think tanks were also interviewed.[2] These accounts are drawn together to tell the story of New Labour's road to the New Deal.

The chapter is structured as follows. It begins with an account of Labour's search for a new identity and its reshaping of economic and welfare policy. In the course of this, the Labour leadership identified and became influenced by new policy models on welfare and social security, which are explored in the next section. That these models became policy practice – as the New Deal programme – within 12 months of Labour taking up office, was facilitated by a process of reform of government administrative structures, which had started in the 1980s and accelerated under Labour. This resulted in a changing balance of power in government administration.

The accounts presented here challenge claims of a paramount influence of the US experience on the UK New Deal. New Labour contributed to changing the language of social security, insisting on referring to *welfare* instead, and

---

[2] During the restructuring of Government Departments in 2001, most staff were directly transferred to the renamed organization. Some departmental units however, were transferred from one Department (DfEE) to another (DWP). Wherever quotations refer to staff, their 'home' Department prior to restructuring and at the time of the interview is indicated.

popularized the concept that a claimant's *rights* to benefits were matched by *responsibilities*, which ensured that public policy objectives could be and were met. Undoubtedly, these changes were borrowed and adopted from the US. However, the US were not the only source of inspiration for policy changes, and the origin of the New Deal can only be properly understood by taking account of, both, external influences and Labour party-internal drivers for change.

New Labour: New Focus and the American Influence

New Labour's assimilation of its political language to that of the party of US Democrats is probably the most widely documented piece of evidence of the transformation of the UK party from *Old* to *New* Labour. The party jettisoned its socialist (*Old* Labour) credentials in favour of a social-democratic orientation, which emphasized concern for opportunity over equality in society, and personal obligation alongside social rights. Although informed by Christian Socialist values (Wilkinson, 1998), New Labour's thinking has echoed that of the New Right on both sides of the Atlantic, notably when it began to voice concern over *welfare dependency* and the alleged adverse behavioural effects of welfare receipt (Deacon, 1996).

The Labour Party's transformation of its ideological outlook, language and policies began after its third successive Westminster election defeat in 1987 and built on the fundamental restructuring of the decision-making processes within the organization. This would eventually open the door to more centralized policy-making within Government and increased the role of policy advisers within the Cabinet and Government Departments, largely replacing the role that left-leaning policy think-tanks held in the 1980s and early 1990s. During the party leadership of Neil Kinnock from 1988, the role of the National Executive Council of the Labour Party in deciding policy was strengthened at the expense of the Labour Party Conference, the traditional venue for deciding policy. In 1994, following the party's fourth successive election defeat in 1992 and the death of its then leader John Smith, Tony Blair was elected Party Leader. Blair

> ...took [electoral reform] a stage further. In doing that it meant that the power of the head office and of the parliamentary party and of the leadership became much stronger, the power of affiliated unions and the conference much weaker (Labour Party MP, interviewed 3 April 2001).

The modernization of the Labour Party opened up the organization to the influences and the thinking of strategists, political managers and new political role models, a large number of whom were US American or influenced by US American politics. Labour enjoyed insider access to Democrat strategists, sharing or exchanging key collaborators, such as Philip Gould who had worked in Arkansas for future US President Bill Clinton's campaign before returning to the Labour Party, and George Stephanopoulos, Communications Director of Clinton's campaign. These connections were instrumental to party reform as, following

Labour's 1992 election defeat, in its search for reform models to improve its chances of being elected at the next opportunity, the party turned to US President Clinton's Democrats for inspiration and guidance. Labour adopted US style canvassing and vote polling; the affinity between New Labour's and the US Democrats' thinking on welfare policy also soon became apparent.

King and Wickham-Jones (1999, p. 65) have noted that 'Clinton had long held (*workfarist*) views' (emphasis added). Under his Presidency, the Personal Responsibility and Work Opportunity Reconciliation Act (PRWORA) was passed in 1996. The Act introduced time-limited welfare and further delegated responsibility for welfare reform to US states. *Workfarism*, i.e. linking the receipt of social security benefit – or, in American terminology *welfare* – to work obligations, took root in New Labour at around the same time as Blair and his Shadow Chancellor, Gordon Brown, began their increasingly more frequent visits to Washington and to the Clinton administration in 1993. In the 1980s, Labour had still opposed the then Conservative Government's policy of stricter regulation of unemployed benefit claims, which made the receipt of social assistance conditional upon active job search and threatened recipients who declined job offers with benefit sanctions. By the early 1990s, New Labour no longer opposed the *stricter benefit regime*, but perceived it as part and parcel of its own welfare programme.

New Labour: Economic Policy and the Domestic Scene

Stricter welfare regulation became acceptable to New Labour because, in the light of US experience at the time, it was felt that greater conditionality was an effective tool for reducing the unemployed claimant count. The party's principal political thinkers argued that increasing job search obligations was also acceptable to the electorate; a view that was confirmed in focus groups, which the Party initiated in the run-up to the 1997 election to gauge public opinion and reactions to New Labour's proposed new policies (Gould, 1999). The concept also found support in the party's shifting economic policy paradigm.

In the early 1990s, the Party's dominant economic thinking abandoned its traditional Keynesian base, as advocated by Cambridge University economists, such as John Eatwell, and moved towards a policy designed on micro-economic principles and promoted by LSE-based economists, Richard Layard and John Philpott. Layard and Philpott were interested in labour market policies to reduce rising levels of long-term unemployment and had studied these policies in Europe and the US. Their research led them to conclude that the long-term unemployed should be offered a guarantee of regular employment in the public or the voluntary sector, as this would facilitate their eventual re-integration into the labour market.

Blair met Layard in the early 1990s, when he was Opposition Spokesperson for Employment. The connection between Layard and Blair was renewed in the mid-1990s, after Layard's return from the lengthy stay abroad. In 1997, finally, Layard became adviser to HM Treasury and one of several policy experts that the party had informally consulted whilst in opposition and subsequently hired to help in the design of the New Labour government's economic and labour market policies. The party's welfare-to-work policy was slowly taking shape over a period of time before the party's arrival in government and in tandem with the party's reform of its economic and fiscal programme.

Layard's thinking had been influenced by the experience of Swedish labour market policy. During the 1980s and again in the latter half of the 1990s, labour market policy in Sweden combined high levels of income security, by paying generous benefits that replaced a large proportion of lost wage income, with a comprehensive system of employment services. At the point of benefit exhaustion after 14 months of unemployment, the unemployed were offered temporary public employment. Layard's research suggested that Sweden's highly active labour market intervention performed better and more effectively than less active policies elsewhere in Europe (Layard et al., 1996). Following the Swedish example, Layard and his colleagues not only advocated the introduction of a job guarantee, but also argued that this guarantee should signify a 'duty to work' as well a 'right to work' (Layard and Philpott, 1991). The *work duty* should be enforced through time-limiting social security benefits. As in Sweden, active labour market policy (ALMP) should replace benefits and not present an 'optional alternative', which in their view, would be more costly (Layard et al., 1996, p. 264). The concept of ALMP proposed by Layard and his colleagues was, thus, not far removed from the present welfare-to-work programme of the New Deal.

Layard and his colleagues first expressed their views on ALMP during the Conservative government in the late 1980s and early 1990s. However, Conservative politicians perceived Layard's and Philpott's employment guarantee as too expensive, because they feared that the public sector might have to step in as a job provider, if the private sector failed to supply sufficient placement opportunities. Despite its reservations, the Conservative Government set up of a high level internal review group to discuss the options open to welfare reform, which included the time-limiting of social security benefits, which, at that time, was being discussed and, ultimately, introduced in the US. In 1996, it also piloted Project Work, which offered long-term unemployed people 13 weeks of job search assistance followed by 13 weeks of mandatory work experience placement (paying benefits plus £10). In the words of one policy adviser (interviewed 16 January 2001), this was 'a very cheapo New Deal', which gave an early indication of the direction into which policy was going to move over the following months.

New Labour turned out to be considerably more receptive to the idea of large-scale job placement programme than the Conservatives had been. It would seem difficult to overestimate the importance of the LSE economists' ideas and the turn-around in policy thinking that they represented, in particular, for the Labour Party. Since the 1970s, the dominant perception within Government Departments had been that prevention of long-term unemployment was key (Price, 2000). An efficiently managed Employment Service was to place individuals, who had recently become unemployed into new jobs, and would do so quickly, before the jobseekers became long-term unemployed and harder to place with employers. Although beneficial to the short-term unemployed, critics argued that this policy inevitably failed the long-term unemployed. Moreover, many short-term unemployed people were believed to be able to find employment without the assistance of the Employment Service. Targeting policies at the short-term unemployed was, therefore, inefficient and carried a high risk of economic *deadweight*.

In contrast to this prevailing policy doctrine, Layard and his colleagues argued that policy should target the long-term unemployed. Their key argument was that refocusing policy on this group of jobseekers would have no detrimental effect on the short-term unemployed, causing little or no displacement. To the contrary, with sufficient effort, it would lift the return-to-work rate of the long-term unemployed to equal that of the short-term unemployed, thus contributing to a general reduction in unemployment.

New Labour accepted Layard's and his colleagues' economic theory, as policymakers[3] and policy analyst inside and outside government soon found out. In fact, policymakers who later became involved in the design and implementation of the New Deal had for some time been aware of New Labour's plans to change Government's active labour market policy and re-target it on the long-term unemployed:

> [The Labour Party] made it perfectly clear, from two or three years before the '97 election, that they intended to put in place a major programme particularly aimed at young, unemployed people, if they won the election... When the 1997 election was going to be, [so] broad lines of Labour party ambition were reasonably clear... They also said...not only will we look after the younger people, we also want to look after the older, and that turned out to be over 50s. So we were perfectly clear that they wanted to have a major programme for these two groups of people. It's perfectly clear, it was going to be linked to the administration of the Jobseeker's Allowance system, benefit system, and it was also clear that it was intended to have an element of compulsion to it... What we decided we needed to do...was that we ought to use, two or three months before the election to work out precisely how you might do this. So in that period between about February and May 1997, we set up a lot of work inside the Department (Policymaker, DfEE, interviewed 8 February 2001).

The New Deal: a Conceptual Hybrid

In the mid-1990s, Labour needed to realign its core policies, in particular on the economy, to 'provide the party with the middle-class support that electoral victory demanded' (King and Wickham-Jones, 1999, p. 67). The coming-together of Blair and Layard, who shared this view, provided the party with the intellectual means to construct a comprehensive welfare-to-work programme that was compatible with Labour's plan to keep spending within the limits set by the Conservative

---

[3] Policymakers are civil servants charged with designing policy programmes and/or implementing larger as well as small, more specific interventions, including the delivery of policy in the regions. Policy analysts, on the other hand, monitor and evaluate interventions and progress in policy implementation, and include specialists, such as labour market analysts.

government. This was intended to reassure the electorate that a New Labour government would not return to old Labour principles of *tax and spend.*

Retaining existing spending limits ruled out the adoption of the Scandinavian model of the welfare state with large-scale public sector resource input, which was viewed by the party leadership as being financially 'unsustainable in the long run' (Labour MP, interviewed 3 April 2001). Moreover, evaluations of UK training programmes in the 1980s and 1990s were suggested such programmes were of limited effectiveness (Machin and Wilkinson, 1995; Robinson, 2000). As a result, 'the Labour party's predilection...for training as a solution to unemployment was getting a fair mauling' (Economic advisor, interviewed 11 January 2002). Large-scale job creation and job training programmes were struck off New Labour's modernist policy agenda.

By contrast, short-term job search and placement programmes, such as Restart and Work Trials[4], appeared to work and, most importantly, appeared to be cost-effective (e.g. White and Lakey, 1992; White et al., 1997).[5] New Labour was advised, and believed, that moving away from training towards welfare-to-work programmes would be more effective and less costly to public finances. One estimate suggested a likely reduction in social security expenditure by up to 18 per cent (King and Wickham-Jones, 1999). These savings would, of course, be lost, or at least substantially reduced, if the public sector was to provide employment for unemployed people who could not find jobs in the private sector.

Policy analysts, in particular within think tanks close to New Labour (for instance, Demos or the Institute for Public Policy Research) were taking firm note of the findings of the US welfare-to-work programme evaluations, in particular those from California's Riverside County (see Chapter 6). These showed that unemployed people could be moved into private sector employment at comparatively low cost to the public sector, welfare caseloads reduced and the earnings of the (formerly) unemployed increased. Such findings strengthened the case for welfare reform and the introduction of welfare-to-work programmes. At the same time as this news was received from the USA, the complementary view gained momentum that there was little to learn from welfare programmes in European countries. In fact, the conviction soon became that Britain had Europe a lot to teach:

> They [the Labour government]...thought that Europe was basically fairly out of date on welfare issues and they would go further than most social democratic parties in Western Europe on cutting back on welfare expenditure. They would buy into the argument that one of the problems of the continental European economy are the high levels of corporate taxation required to fund a very strong welfare state (Labour Party MP, interviewed 3 April 2001).

---

[4] Three-week trial placement with prospective employers, during which jobseekers continue to receive their benefits and can also have expenses covered.
[5] Project Work however, was revealed to have only been a limited success (Bryson et al., 1998).

The US model offered an alternative to continental European models, and in particular the Swedish model, which was compatible with the UK's comparatively low-spending social security system. Unlike Sweden, but like the US, welfare-to-work in the UK would focus on enforcing programme participation, whilst maintaining the low benefit payments and low replacement rates. Like Sweden, but unlike the US, UK welfare-to-work was also going to be universal and, for most unemployed benefit claimants, mandatory. The US evidence appeared to suggest that jobs could be found in the private sector and there was no need to rely on costly public sector employment, as had been the case in Sweden.

Within New Labour, the Swedish model was still disliked for the role it assigned to the public sector, which the political hierarchy did not believe, would have gained the support of the electorate. However, New Labour could not and, in fact, did not want to do away with the principle of inclusive provision and welfare-to-work assistance for all. The way to overcome this dilemma of running a comprehensive welfare-to-work programme on low cost was to draw in the support of the private business sector, as US welfare-to-programmes had done, but at a larger scale. This required a representational shift and a greater emphasis on the principle of *rights and responsibilities*, which would ensure benefit claimants' compliance with the emerging welfare and benefits regime, which strictly enforced active job search, but would also appeal to the more conservative voter and, in particular, the business sector.

> If you'd just gone down the Swedish model...it would have been far more an anathema to Blair who was re-positioning away from an emphasis on the public sector as the employer of last resort...with the public sector as the major deliverer. And the *rights and responsibilities* language was just up Layard's street...It just fitted well with his own re-positioning of the party, but still despite that...it involved the US language (Economic adviser, interviewed 11 January 2002).

In its 1996 *Road to the manifesto* publication on social security (Labour Party, 1996), Labour still referred to its policy as 'benefit-to-work' (Labour Party, 1996, p. 2) and avoided reference to welfare-to-work, which was more firmly rooted in the US language. By 1997, when Labour published its election document *New deal for a New Britain*, the language had changed and the party's reform proposals were now referred to as 'our welfare-to-work programme' (Labour Party, 1997, p. 2).

Early signs of the eventual adoption of more regulatory welfare policy and sanctioning were, however, already apparent in the 1996 document. The document drew more heavily on the Australian experience, advocating a model similar to the Australian Jobs, Education and Training (JET) programme for the UK, than on US experience. Labour pledged to introduce a JET scheme for Britain, improving co-ordination of Departmental and agency activities and providing unemployed people with 'job advocates' (Labour Party, 1996, p. 3) along the line of Job Advisors in Australia. In a departure from the JET model, which was voluntary, however, Labour foresaw its own programme to be mandatory:

Where it is clear that a claimant is unreasonably refusing a suitable offer Labour will have no hesitation in imposing a benefit penalty, as in the present system, of a 40 per cent reduction in payments (Labour Party, 1996, p. 2).

New Deal – New Players

In the mid-1980s, the Employment Service became the driver-designate of claimant activation in the UK. From Restart in the mid-1980s to Project Work in 1996, the Employment Service, reorganized as an Executive Agency in 1990, had built up expertise in policing as well as delivering unemployment benefits. The Service was seen as delivering on its dual responsibilities with considerable effect, particularly after 1990 when *active signing* was introduced, which required unemployment benefit claimants to provide evidence of their job search efforts. From that point, claimants could be referred to advisers who would seek to enforce active job search. The Employment Service's approach was based on the reasoning that:

> You pay people benefits and so, therefore, you use the administration to stop benefit dependency building up and the disincentives. You get people to act as if they're not getting benefits (Policy Analyst, DfEE, interviewed 14 February 2001).

The principles of active signing were further developed with the introduction of the Jobseeker's Allowance in 1996, which included a Jobseeker's Agreement to be signed by all benefit recipients. Jobseeker's Agreements between claimants and their Employment Service adviser spelt out the job search activities that the claimant was expected to undertake. They also provided the bases for decisions to sanction claimants for non-compliance. Jobseeker's Allowance later proved a crucial prerequisite to the New Deal by providing legitimacy to making programme participation mandatory for specific target groups:

> JSA certainly paved the way for a much more active labour market policy and it provided a legal framework, which allowed an adviser-based intervention to operate (Policymaker, DfEE, interviewed 22 November 2000).

The reduction of eligibility for *contributory* unemployment benefit, which is paid regardless of need or means, from 12 months to six months under the 1996 JSA legislation subsequently became the basis – or justification – for requiring medium-term unemployed people to participate in the New Deal for Young People (NDYP).

Although the Employment Service strongly promoted and influenced the outcome of these changes, the Service had not always been in the driving seat of active labour market policy. Over the decades, it had struggled with the Department of Health and Social Security (DHSS, later the Department of Social Security) over their respective roles in administering benefits and preventing benefit fraud, and assisting and policing claimants' job search activities (Price,

2000; King, 1995). In the mid- to late-1970s, the Employment Service still perceived its main role as serving employers by helping to fill job vacancies and it showed little interest in linking the administration of unemployment benefit with its job placement activities. This changed in the 1980s when the Department of Employment, under whose auspices the Employment Service fell at that time, made 'a takeover bid, with Ministerial backing, to handle [means-tested Supplementary Benefit] as well as [Unemployment Benefit] for the unemployed' (Price, 200, p. 210). The DHSS was defensive, fearing for the coherence of the social security system if they were to lose administrative control over supplementary benefits. In the end, when the DHSS was split into DSS and DoH in 1988, DSS retained responsibility for income support (the successor to Supplementary Benefit) and, later, means-tested Jobseeker's Allowance. Although it lost its battle over the benefits, Employment Service remained convinced that it should provide JSA personal advisers under the new active-signing regime, because it already had substantial experience in providing personal advice in employment offices and Jobcentres.

In 2001, finally, the Employment Service became part of the re-organized and renamed Department for Work and Pensions (DWP). This process united the administration of contributory and means-tested Jobseeker's Allowance in one organization, structured according to claimants' life-phases (Families and Children, Working Age, and Pensions and Retirement) rather than by type of benefit. It also consolidated the roles and positions of personal advisers in Jobcentres within the new DWP.

While DfEE was the main driving force behind moves to integrate the administration of benefits and the provision of employment services, the DSS was initially reluctant to join in these efforts. Arguably, differences between the DfEE and the DSS were overcome, when Her Majesty's Treasury Department emerged as a new and, ultimately, the main player in UK social policy with New Labour's arrival in office. The Treasury sought to reform welfare policy in order 'to find some device for neutralizing the natural tendencies of any new left-of-centre government to use public expenditure in pursuit of its objectives' (Deakin and Parry, 2000, p. 186). Chancellor Brown preferred 'low-cost social policy' (Deakin and Parry, 2000, p. 193) and increased work incentives, and disliked passive labour market policy that risked increasing (benefit) spending unless tied to activation.

With financial considerations paramount, active and costly public sector involvement in the provision of job placements needed to be kept to a minimum. This left encouraging and monitoring participants' active job search and the primacy of unsubsidized private sector employment at the core of the New Deal, while maintaining the programme's universality:

> You needed to link the benefit payment and the job-search…the focus on the sort of one stop shop that has benefit on job-search is…it's cheap. And you deal with everybody… If your cheapest intervention is also your best you might as well give it to everybody, which is basically and actually the way we've done it in the UK. Even more…we actually get the individuals to do all the work themselves. It's like self-service. The Jobseeker's Agreement says you will go out and do this, not

necessarily in the job centre. So the line that we take…is we help all of the people all of the time, and you differentiate by duration (Policy Analyst, interviewed 14 February 2001).

New Labour still faced the problem of raising the resources necessary to fund the administration and the subsidized-job option of the New Deal. Meeting the needs of those jobseekers that failed to obtain regular employment after placements in subsidized employment, the voluntary option and the Environment Task Force was still going to be expensive as was the provision of personalized services. The solution that Chancellor Brown found was to impose a one-off *Windfall Tax* on the profits of national industries and utility companies, which had been privatized during the previous decade or two. Although retrospective taxation was procedurally highly unusual, Brown was able successfully to capitalize on popular opinion prevalent at the time that national assets had been sold below their market value and that imposing a retrospective tax was, for this reason, justified (Chennels, 1997).

From Welfare-to-Work to Workfare?

The New Deal programme was informed by a Swedish prototype, influenced by positive UK and US experience of strict job-search enforcement and sanctioning for non-compliance, shaped by the constraints of the UK's low-cost welfare regime and supported ideologically by the perceived threat of welfare dependency. But to what extent did the New Deal represent policy innovation?

In his 1991 study, Walker discovered many features of US welfare-to-work programmes present in the then prevailing UK system of active labour market policies:

> Many of the schemes which have been experimented with locally in the United States are available nationally in Britain. At any one time the Youth Training and Employment Training schemes will be providing primarily on-the-job training for 360,000 and 210,000 people respectively. 'Back to work plans' are agreed with all people signing on as unemployed. There is systematic follow-up and reinterviewing of those who do not take up a place on an employment or training programme when they had agreed to do so. An 'advisory interview' after 13 weeks of unemployment is held with selected clients who are unable to find employment when their skills are in demand locally. The Restart programme provides an interview for all people unemployed for six months which is often followed by attendance on an 'Options' course or participation in a job club. Claimants who cannot demonstrate that they are actively seeking work may have their benefit suspended for one or two weeks. Similarly, people who have been unemployed for two or more years and refuse to attend an Options course stand to lose a proportion of their benefit for a period equivalent to the length of the course. Young people who refuse places on Youth Training may lose their right to receive income support (Walker, 1991, p. 50).

Since then, the New Deal has added three new dimensions. First, active labour market policy has extended its reach beyond the short-term unemployed towards the long-term unemployed. Secondly, it has sought to integrate a diverse range of principally interconnected, but in practice separately administered, programmes under one heading. Thirdly, it has added to the degree of compulsion and given primacy to employment in the private sector.

Casting the Net Wider – But Not Too Wide

The face of unemployment changed in the 1980s and the 1990s. First, the proportion of long-term unemployment rose as successive post-recession economic recoveries failed to make noticeable inroads into reducing the stock of people unemployed for one year or longer. Secondly, the pool of the unemployed was becoming more diverse. Whereas in the 1970s and 1980s, unemployment was largely concentrated among occupational groups and former employees of declining industries, most notably in manufacturing and mining, this changed in the late 1980s and 1990s. The end of the Lawson Boom generated sudden increases in unemployment amongst service sector employees. In other words, unemployment was no longer confined to declining industrial areas, although it remained higher in those areas than elsewhere. Hence, area-based initiatives, which had been used widely to alleviate the geographical concentration of unemployment, were becoming less appropriate. In addition, youth unemployment came to be seen as a problem for public policy, which could not be resolved through conventional training or retraining programmes.

Against this background of change, unemployment was to be addressed not programmatically through job creation measures, but administratively through activation measures. In order to cater for an increasingly diverse unemployed labour force, the New Deal was to cast its net wider, although financial constraints precluded a programme that would cater for all, short-term and long-term, unemployed. The New Deal's emphasis on *activating* the long-term unemployed in general, and young unemployed people in particular, reflected the need to focus resources and to target them at those, whose experience of unemployment was most likely to have an adverse effect on future employment prospects:

> The difference [to previous programmes] was... First of all, the labour proposal was absolutely, explicitly, about 18-24 year olds. And, secondly, that eligibility for these schemes started after people had been unemployed for a relatively short period...Most of the earlier experiments with things, which are in the family of the New Deal, were confined to people who've been unemployed for two years...They weren't particularly targeted at youth unemployment, they were targeted at long term unemployment... The New Deal was an altogether bigger, more ambitious, more specifically targeted, more clearly defined programme than we'd seen before. The scale of it exceeded anything that we'd done before and the concreteness, the specific conditions of the New Deal, was more ambitious (Policymaker, HM Treasury, interviewed 21 May 2001).

Integration and Packaging

A major part of the political success of New Labour's welfare reform programme was the way it had been *packaged* and presented to the public. The core of the policy was to integrate a diverse set of existing programmes under one heading. But, while integration was perceived to be necessary because of the diversity of clients that personal advisers were expected to have to deal with, it also had important promotional benefits:

> [In the US,] there's nothing really equivalent for the sort of New Deal *brand image*, which, these days, in terms of getting messages across and things meaning something to employers as well as unemployed people…is quite important (Government minister, interviewed 23 March 2001; emphasis added).

Packaging programmes and creating a brand image allowed New Labour in opposition and, later, in government to sell a product to the private sector, whom it relied upon as the main deliverer of jobs. It provided the opportunity to extend the rhetoric of *rights and responsibilities*, of cohesion and mutuality, to industry, which was offered a public service and, in return, was expected to make use of it.

Compulsion and Private Sector Employment

The issue of compulsion has received much attention among students of recent developments in active labour market policy in the UK. For instance, Peck and Theodore have argued that:

> Perhaps the most significant single 'lesson' learned from America concerns the role of compulsion, although arguably this has been more of a political lesson than a programming one, given that the US evaluation evidence on work compulsion remains inconclusive (Peck and Theodore, 2001, p. 450).

In fact, UK interest in compulsion can be traced back to Conservative Government policy in the 1980s (Dolowitz, 1997). However, at that time, it was felt that the electorate would not accept the receipt of social security benefits made strictly conditional upon active job search or upon the acceptance of work, irrespective of the pay it might offer.

US welfare-to-work programmes, which UK politicians and policymakers in the early 1990s were familiar with, still strongly relied on public sector involvement as the provider of employment or work placements. Although this was beginning to change, such programmes provided few role models for the UK, while the Conservative (Major) Government remained reluctant to invest heavily in welfare-to-work programmes. For the same reason, the Government also disliked proposals, such as put forward by Layard and his colleagues, which were built on the principle of the public sector as the *employer of last resort*, that is, as a key provider of job placements. Because compulsion, in turn, was perceived to put the public sector into exactly that position of *employer of last resort*, if the private sector failed to provide sufficient numbers of new jobs or job placement opportunities, Conservative efforts to make welfare more punitive finally stalled.

New Labour's linking of compulsion with the notion of the private sector taking the lead in welfare-to-work policy was a lesson learned from more recent US initiatives and reinforced by Swedish and Australian experience. All three suggested that active job search in the private sector could yield positive results by moving people off benefit.

US welfare-to-work programmes had mainly dealt with lone parents and, in terms of their client groups, were, therefore, much more homogenous than similar programmes would need to be in the UK. For this reason, policymakers and politicians were largely sceptical about the transferability of US programmes to the UK. However, their attitude towards *learning* lessons from the experience of US welfare-to-work programmes was becoming increasingly positive. This was well illustrated by the shifting of attitudes, during the early and late 1990s, of House of Commons Select Committees. Scepticism towards welfare-to-work/workfare programmes and continued support for training programmes (House of Common Employment Committee, 1993-1995) was overtaken by a belief that the US experience had shown that 'welfare can be an active programme' and 'self-sufficiency [through welfare-to-work programmes] was feasible' (House of Commons Social Security Select Committee, 1997-1998). In a virtual circle, compulsion and punitive welfare became more acceptable to the UK because US welfare-to-work appeared to work, and it appeared to work because of compulsion.

The question arises whether the New Deal is in fact a case of *Workfare*. The answer clearly depends on how W*orkfare* is defined. Narrowly defined it signifies 'working for benefits' or 'working for benefits plus', that is, benefits supplemented with contributions towards claimants' cost of travelling to work and other of their work-related expenses. This is not typically the case in the New Deal, which seeks to help participants earn a wage.

> It was quite clear as well that the government was not going down a *Workfare* route. It was not categorically, not trying to set up a structure that required activity, however pointless, however little it was adding to an individual's portfolio. On the contrary, it was saying, we do wish to pursue and require a full-time activity route. But we want that full-time activity route to be significant in terms of its ability to enhance, and likelihood of enhancing, an individual's portfolio, in terms of being an active player in the labour market, someone who is trying to sell his services, her services, to an employer (Policymaker, DfEE, interviewed 31 October 2000).

Whether the New Deal can (continue to) steer away from becoming *Workfare* will depend on the extent of the private sector's participation in the programme and the placement and employment opportunities that it offers. Efforts in recent years to extend compulsory participation in the New Deal to lone parents (now required to attend a work-focused interview, but not required to participate in the New Deal) and to disabled people (participation still voluntary), and increasing enforcement of active job search requirements by personal advisers in the new Jobcentre Plus offices might put a strain on this contribution.

Policymakers have argued that

> The word *Workfare* would never have been mentioned by us, but it would have been something that ministers would have wanted us to work towards, but in as quiet a way as possible (Policymaker, DfEE, interviewed 6 June 2001).

If private sector employment were ever to fall short of meeting programme demand for job placements, the public sector might have to take on the role of the *employer of last resort*. At that point, the New Deal would move a step closer to *Workfare*.

Conclusion

UK welfare policy has undergone a major transformation not just under New Labour, but also under previous Conservative Governments. Politicians' and policymakers' concerns about *benefit dependency*, which, in their view, would result from the unconditional receipt of social security benefit, were the driving force behind this transformation.

The UK's New Deal differs from the US welfare-to-work programmes in several respects. First, it offers near universal coverage of the unemployed population, whereas provisions in the US remain highly segmented, offering little social assistance to the unemployed. Secondly, the New Deal is informed by principles of *solidarity* and is an acknowledgement of the state's responsibility towards the citizen, as much as the New Deal also is an expression of citizen's responsibilities towards the state. The underlying notion of solidarity is much less apparent in the US, where welfare-to-work policies have primarily the result of concerns about the cost of welfare provision and the spectre of the (black) *underclass*.

Moreover, unlike welfare-to-work programmes in the US, the UK New Deal was part and parcel of efforts to *integrate* public policy. Integration would bring together new welfare policy objectives with an active labour market policy in a way, which previous Conservative governments had feared might become too expensive for the public sector to fund. Integration would also create a more comprehensive welfare system, supported by further measures, such as the National Minimum Wage and, most recently, the introduction of Tax Credit, designed to provide in-work support for families and individuals with low or medium earnings. This integration is in stark contrast to the US model of welfare, whose reform process promoted diversity. As a result, the US welfare system has remained highly fragmented, while its continued policy focus on lone parents has prevented the emergence of wider, perhaps universal coverage.

New Labour's thinking on the New Deal started from the perspective of labour market policy and the lessons learned about the relative ineffectiveness of traditional job training programmes for the (long-term) unemployed. These lessons emanated, almost simultaneously, from Europe (in particular, Sweden) and the US. However, unlike the European lessons, which mainly confirmed the limitation of training programmes, evidence from the US also offered an alternative concept: moving unemployed individuals directly and quickly into jobs was working well in reducing the benefit caseloads.

The New Deal was the product of external policy learning and of the adoption of a new economic theory by New Labour. Its implementation took place within strict parameters set by the party's commitment to maintain the previous Government's spending commitments. Yet, New Labour managed to circumnavigate these parameters when it introduced the Windfall Tax.

In preparing and articulating its new position of welfare and welfare reform, New Labour drew on expert advice. At later stages, when details of the New Deal were worked out and the programme was finally launched, the party also relied on civil servants' operational expertise and their practical knowledge of policymaking. The latter's role is the subject of the next chapter.

References

Bryson, A., Lissenburgh, S. and Payne, J. (1998), *The First Project Work Pilots: A quantitative evaluation*, Report to the Employment Service and the Department for Education and Employment, Policy Studies Institute, London.

Chennels, L. (1997), 'The Windfall Tax', *Fiscal Studies*, vol. 18.3, pp. 279-291.

Deacon, A. (1996), 'Welfare and character' in F. Field (ed.) *Stakeholder Welfare*, Institute of Economic Affairs, London.

Dolowitz, D. (1997), 'British employment policy in the 1980s: learning from the American experience', *Governance: An International Journal of Policy and Administration*, vol. 10.1, pp. 23-42.

Gould, P. (1999), *The Unfinished Revolution: How the Modernisers Saved the Labour Party*, Abacus, London.

Hamilton, G. and Friedlander, D. (1989), *Final Report on the Saturation Work Initiative Model in San Diego*, Manpower Demonstration Research Corporation, New York.

Hasluck, C., McKnight, A. and Elias, P. (2000), *Evaluation of the New Deal for Lone Parents: Early Lessons from the Phase One Prototype – Synthesis Report*, Department of Social Security Research Report No. 110, Corporate Document Services, Leeds.

King, D. and Wickham-Jones, M. (1999), 'From Clinton to Blair: The Democratic (Party) Origins of welfare to work', *Political Quarterly*, vol. 70.1, pp. 62-74.

Labour Party (1996), *Getting Welfare to Work: A New Vision for Social Security*, The Labour Party, London.

Labour Party (1997), *New Deal for a New Britain – Labour's Proposals to Tackle Youth and Long-term Unemployment*, The Labour Party, London.

Layard, R. with Jackman, R. and Nickell, S. (1996), *Combating Unemployment: Is Flexibility Enough?*. Macroeconomic Policies and Structural Reform, OECD, Paris, pp. 19-49 (reproduced in R. Layard (1999), Tackling Unemployment, Macmillan: Basingstoke).

Layard, R. and Philpott, J. (1991), *Stopping Unemployment*, The Employment Institute, London.

Machin, S. and Wilkinson, D. (1995), *Employee Training: Unequal Access and Economic Performance*, Institute for Public Policy Research, London.

Mulgan, G. (1998), *'Is UK Welfare Reform a Copycat Exercise?'* in W.J. Wilson, G. Mulgan, J. Hills and D. Piachaud, Welfare Reform: Learning from American Mistakes? Report of a seminar organised by LSE Housing and CASE, CASE Report No.3, Centre for the Analysis of Social Exclusion, London, pp. 22-30.

OECD (1996), *The OECD Jobs Study: Implementing the Strategy*, OECD, Paris.

Peck, J. and Theodore, N. (2001), 'Exporting Workfare/Importing Welfare-to-Work: Exploring the Politics of Third Way Policy Transfer', *Political Geography*, Vol. 20, pp. 427-460.

Price, D. (2000), *Office of Hope. A History of the Employment Service*, Policy Studies Institute, London.

Riley, R. and Young, G. (2000), *The New Deal for Young People: Implications for Employment and the Public Finances*, Research & Development Report ESRC62, Employment Service, Sheffield.

Robinson, P. (2000), 'Active Labour-Market Policies: A Case of Evidence-Based Policy-Making?', *Oxford Review of Economic Policy*, vol. 16.1, pp. 13-26.

Tonge, J. (1999), 'New Packaging, Old Deal? New Labour and Employment Policy Innovation', *Critical Social Policy*, vol. 59, 19:2, pp. 217-232.

TUC (2002), *New Deal – An Occasional Briefing*. Number 65 (14 February). Trades Union Congress, London.

Weaver, R. K. (2000), *Ending Welfare as We Know It*, Brookings Institution Press, Washington.

Wiseman, M. (2000), 'Making work for welfare in the United States', in I. Lodemel and H. Trickey (eds.) *'An Offer you can't refuse'. Workfare in International Perspective*, The Policy Press, Bristol.

Wilkinson, A. (1998), *Christian Socialism: Scot Holland to Tony Blair*, SCM Press, London.

White, M and Lakey, J. (1992), *The Restart Effect. Does Active Labour Market Policy Reduce Unemployment?*, Policy Studies Institute, London.

White, M., Lissenburgh, S. and Bryson, A. (1997), *The Impact of Public Job Placing Programmes*, Policy Studies Institute, London.

Chapter 3

The Use of Evidence in the Design of the 'New Deal'

Andreas Cebulla

[It] seemed to be the right way to move forward (Policymaker, DSS, interviewed 8 November 2000).

Introduction

When introduced in 1997, the UK's New Deal appeared to present a break from a pattern of fragmented experimentation and programming of active labour market policies of the previous decade. The New Deal was a seemingly coherent package of targeted and customized policy initiatives under one heading, albeit two different administrations: the Department of Social Security (DSS, now the Department for Work and Pensions) and the Department for Education and Employment (DfEE, now the Department for Education and Skills). This integration of various strands of labour market policies under one heading meant that the roots of the New Deal lay in past experience of policymaking as well as the introduction of new ideas and economic concepts (see Chapter 2).

In this chapter, the search, within the civil service, for evidence of workable and seemingly effective active labour market projects and programmes that would finally inform the design of the New Deal is explored. Weiss and Bucuvalas (1980, p .140) have usefully distinguished in their work between instrumental and conceptual purposes of using research. It is the former, instrumental use of research that is of interest to this chapter, following on from the previous chapter's investigation of the conceptual use of research. The latter explored and assessed the role of New Labour changing political and economic policy and that of politicians and their advisors in shaping the New Deal. The present chapter focuses on the role, contribution and methods of policy makers and policy analysts.

A central issue of this exploration is the extent to which national and international evidence has interacted to inform the design of the New Deal. More specifically, we examine how this evidence was gathered, interpreted, presented and incorporated into the programme's design. Because the influence of US American evidence on the New Deal is often mentioned as specifically important, it will also be discussed in this chapter.

As in the previous Chapter, the analysis builds on the information gathered in a series of face-to-face and telephone interviews with policy makers and policy analysts in three key government Departments: the then Departments of Social Security and for Education and Employment, and HM Treasury. In total, nineteen interviews were conducted between July 2000 and April 2001, with another one added in January 2002. All interviews, therefore, took place before the restructuring of the Departments in April 2002. The Departments will be referred to by their titles at the time of the interviews.

The sections that follow illustrate how, in the eyes of policymakers and policy analysts[6], the New Deal did not represent a radical departure from existing policy practice. Rather, it was a refinement, which built on both domestic experience and the gathering of evidence about successful policy models internationally. Much of the international information was obtained from the US, yet only selected elements of US welfare-to-work programmes directly informed the design and implementation of the New Deal. 'Negative evidence' – the perception that current and past labour market policies were no longer adequate and could no longer serve the needs of a changing, increasingly complex economy and labour force – was one of the driving forces behind the implementation of the New Deal. 'Negative evidence' also circumscribed the shape that the New Deal could take, or rather: not take. The outcome was a greater emphasis placed on the conditionality of benefit payments, that is, the expectation that benefit claimants would seek and accept paid work as quickly as possible. Both, domestic and international evidence suggested that this approach would be most successful in reducing unemployment and the duration of unemployment. Domestic and international experience and case studies provided illustrations as how such an approach may best be delivered.

Development of Policy and Policy-Making

Deacon (2000) has suggested that the rapid implementation of job search policy in UK before anywhere else in Europe 'is a reflection of the greater influence of American ideas in the UK' (Deacon 2000, p.13). There is little disputing that exposure to US active labour market policies has had a major impact on the thinking of policy-shapers and policy-makers in the UK. This said, the previous chapter has cautioned readers to be aware of other sources of domestic and international thinking that played their role in the decisions to bring in the New Deal and how this programme would look like. Moreover, policy makers and analysts in Britain, while aware of US programmes, also drew on their knowledge

---

[6] We use the term policymaker to describe those civil servants charged with designing policy programmes and/or implementing larger as well as small, more specific interventions, including the delivery of policy in the regions. Policy analysts, on the other hand, monitor and evaluate interventions and progress in policy implementation, and include specialists, such as labour market analysts.

of domestic employment and welfare policies, thereby creating a counterbalance to the growing US influence on policy shaping in this country.

New Labour's plan for a New Deal, while evolving haphazardly in the course of the publication of a series of policy statements and programmes, had taken a fixed form by the time of the May 1997 election. New Labour had carefully planned the New Deal, including estimating its cost implications in advance of announcing it as the main item on its agenda for labour market policy. In the view of some policymakers, the New Deal was a fait-accompli well before it reached the echelons of the British civil service, and this clearly set the frame from within which civil servants could search for implementation ideas and guidelines:

> We thought a bit about suggestions that we might make, but basically it was very easy. Because the proposals were given and they were completely explicit, quite clear, there was no issue about them. The government was committed to implement them, and so we assumed they would be implemented and got on with it as it were (Policymaker, HM Treasury, interviewed 21 May 2001).

About three months before the 1997 election, civil servants were already in contact with New Labour, exploring, discussing and sometimes fine-tuning the party's ideas for the New Deal. It was during this period and in the hectic months following New Labour's election that the New Deal took shape as a 'genuine' programme departing from previous more fragmented efforts at policy programming. During this time, the 'policy-shapers' (that is, politicians and policy-makers) congregated to merge their ideas and understandings of policy concepts and processes in efforts to design and fine-tune a programme that was feasible to implement and likely to be effective.

New Labour's focus on the New Deal as one of its key election pledges meant that it was shaped by politicians rather than by civil servants. The evolution of policy making of previous years, albeit never systematic, from conception to experimentation, or piloting to implementation or abandonment was replaced by the 'grand new idea'. Yet, at that moment in time, the 'grand new idea' also presented an opportunity to develop expertise in policy-making that had until then been more intention than reality.

Home-Grown and Evidence-Based?

Details of the New Deal's structure and activities were discussed and assembled by a working group based within DfEE and also involving the DSS. This working group, having been handed the broad outlines of the New Deal, set about constructing the specifics of the New Deal by adding features already tried in UK employment policy, but never at such a scale. In so doing, it relied on the collective knowledge of employment programmes of some of its longest serving and most experienced civil servants.

Working group members 'examined whether [the New Deal] was justifiable in terms of national and international evidence' (Policy analyst, DfEE, interviewed 14 February 2001). This added to the multiplicity of evidence of existing programmes' effectiveness. The main outcome of this information gathering was to re-enforce a perception that had already prevailed for some time on the basis of the experience of small-scale case studies and pilot programmes, namely that case management and, increasingly, instant job placement were key to successful active labour market policies. The New Deal was to bring together these experiences in one new programme. Unsurprisingly, the view emerged among policy-makers that 'there is nothing even vaguely new in the New Deal...none of the individual bits are new' (Policymaker, DFES, interviewed 22 November 2000) and that:

> The whole of the kind of New Deals should be seen in the context of the employment programmes...that have been developing and a lot of the employment programmes that we have now do have roots in previous programmes...New Deals just didn't quite appear out of nowhere (Policy analyst, DSS, interviewed 21 May 2001).

The civil servants' main contribution to the development of the New Deal was to supply ministers with the detailed technical knowledge required for the effective implementation of the programme. Party officials were concerned with the principles of the New Deal, but were less clear about the substance and detail of the initiative.

In fact, as was argued not least by the Conservative Party politicians we interviewed, New Labour's politicians merely adopted the previous government's view that labour market policy ought to place a greater emphasis on activation, that is, on job search and stronger requirements on unemployed and benefit claimants to be demonstrably available for work. New Labour's review of programmes internationally also led its planners to favour efforts to couple benefits and employment services.

The process by which this detail was collated led some civil servants, including those involved in the design of the New Deal, to the view that the programme was very much 'home-grown', set within the context of coherent programming and joined-up initiatives. However, this view is correct only in so far that the civil servants' collective knowledge of 'what works' or 'what works best' had evolved from earlier programmes and pilot programmes that operated within the UK. Yet, at least some of this knowledge was the product of 'ideas scouting' abroad, above all in the United States and Australia (Finn, 1999: Johnson and Tonkiss, 2002). In other words, the concepts were not necessarily all home-grown. Nevertheless, those that made it into the New Deal had already been tested in the UK. However, as will be shown below, not all had, in fact, proven to be effective.

Moreover, the selection of part of the elements that would later form the New Deal was not only influenced by the principal framework set by New Labour, but also directly by the continued presence of specialist policy advisers to the Labour Party during its discussions with civil servants, in particular after the 1997 election. The fine-tuning of the New Deal was still a two-way process involving,

Welfare-to-Work

on the one hand, the ideas and concepts of politicians and their advisers and, on the other hand, the experiences of Departmental policymakers and policy analysts.

Awareness of Welfare-to-Work Evidence

Since the 1980s, the composition of the unemployed, who were typically former manual workers in declining industries or young job starters, had begun to change and a more diverse client group had emerged that included lone parents, people with disabilities and service sector workers. This greater diversity was one of the reasons for the more frequent piloting of new training and employment programmes, which had begun under the previous Conservative government. The New Deal built on the need for programme structures to reflect the fact that different client groups require different services.

Developing a large-scale programme, such as the New Deal, and the political desire to integrated as yet fragmented policies and their implementing bodies brought with it a re-alignment of policy structures and new structures of co-operation and co-ordination. Charged with employment policy, the DfEE had traditionally been highly aware of labour market policies in other countries. The DSS, on the other hand, harboured specialist knowledge of benefit administration within the UK. The New Deal was to bring this expertise together. Yet, specific knowledge of modern designs of active labour market policies was highly concentrated among selected individuals in both Departments, who were brought together in a working group charged with designing the New Deal.

Within the DSS, expertise largely focussed on domestic programmes. The Jobseeker's Allowance (JSA) and its evaluations (Mackay et al., 1999; Smith et al., 2000) had a profound impact on the thinking of policymakers and policy analysts in the Department. JSA had strengthened benefit claimants' obligation to actively seek employment, introducing the 'job agreement', which unemployed benefit claimants had to sign, as well as reducing the period of non-means-tested JSA eligibility from 12 to six months. The universal introduction of personal advisers was seen as a major success of JSA and was to be retained in the New Deal. Beyond the findings from the JSA evaluation, however, awareness of evaluation evidence, especially systematic awareness, was described by one person as 'peripheral in terms of influencing the way that the shape of the service is' (Policymaker, DSS, interviewed 8 November 2000).

In contrast to the domestic focus of the DSS, DfEE policy makers had earlier exposure to international experience and best-practice, going back to the early 1990s. Unlike their counterparts in the DSS, DfEE officials claimed early awareness of US welfare-to-work programmes, most notably in New York, Wisconsin and, especially, California (GAIN). They also had learned about the Australian Job Compact for the long-term unemployed, which included front line gateway services provided by case managers (cp. Finn, 1997) and upon which the UK New Deal modelled its Single Gateway.

Awareness from Literature

The most critical source of reference, certainly for DfEE/Employment Service policy thinking, however, was the OECD. Its Job Study (OECD, 1996) was seen to provide crucial evidence concerning the effectiveness of new approaches to active labour market policy. The OECD report had praised the UK for its new, more determined active policy measures, exemplified by Restart interviews and job clubs. UK administrators took the praise they received from the OECD as encouragement to continue with their policies and policy reforms. The arguments, however, were circular. UK civil servants had provided the information upon which the OECD then based its assessment of UK labour market policy. Little, if any, further independent evidence was available to substantiate the OECD judgement, and, at the time, only the Restart programme had been evaluated and its findings published (White and Lakey, 1992).

Policymakers rather than policy analysts drove most gathering of information about welfare-to-work programmes and other activation measures. The role of researchers within DSS and DfEE in the early stages of the New Deal was, across the board, described as peripheral. Researchers in DfEE were described as mainly 'reactive' at the time (Policy analyst, DSS, interviewed 21 May 2001), whereas policymakers were 'quite visionary' and also well informed about US literature.' (ibid). As the varied evidence of the effectiveness of new models of active labour market policy was being collected, a uniform, agreed approach to using this information was still lacking. Instead, gathering, presenting and interpreting information about international experiences was very much an individualized activity, providing scope for the shared (but idiosyncratic) use of evidence.

> We have an awful lot of resources, both in terms of the results of former evaluations etc...and also in the skulls of the people who work for the Department. There's a lot of experience and knowledge, and I don't think we tap it particularly systematically (Policymaker, DfEE, interviewed 8 February 2001).

Under these conditions, it was easy, if not inevitable, for individual, well known research projects and studies – above all the OECD Job Study and the US GAIN welfare-to-work experiment – to gain the status of the principal authoritative sources of evidence about effective active labour market policy:

> I go round and knock it out of a potted history, or we use existing documents like *all the evidence and explanations from the OECD* and a variety of different books (Policy analyst, DfEE, interviewed 14 February 2001, emphasis added).

More critical, or perhaps more sceptical, commentators noted that information gathering still resembled 'occasional splurges of interest of actually trying really hard to look across the [board]' (Policymaker, DfEE, interviewed 8 November 2000).

The problem that policy makers and analysts faced when seeking to access information and ideas about welfare-to-work programmes is underlined by the limited volume of reading material addressing these issues that were stored in DSS and DfEE libraries until the mid-1990s. A search of the two main libraries of the DSS and the DfEE produced a total of 129 books or articles that were listed under the keywords 'welfare-to-work' or 'workfare' (Figure 3.1).[7] This excluded UK government publications for instance, statistical and policy reports, such as those produced by the Social Security and the Education Select Committees. The count, however, also included 13 MDRC reports. MDRC is the most prominent evaluator of US welfare-to-work programmes and perhaps the US organization with the highest profile in the UK.

Most of the publications in these libraries had been published in either 1997 (31) or 1998 (19).[8] Although these publication dates can only serve as a proxy for their acquisition date, they nevertheless give some indication of the increasing importance to the two Departments of obtaining information about welfare-to-work programmes around and just after the time that New Labour entered government and the New Deal was introduced.[9]

Notably, among the 50 works published in 1997 and 1998 and acquired by the DSS or the DfEE library, only two were MDRC publications. The remainder were secondary analyses or descriptive reports of welfare-to-work programmes rather than MDRC-style evaluations or evaluation summaries.

The DfEE library (68) held a few more welfare-to-work relevant publications than the DSS library (61). However, this was largely due to DfEE's library 'catching up' quickly from about 1997 onwards, when it acquired the majority of publications counted in this exercise. This appeared to reflect the increasing importance of welfare-to-work issues to the DfEE and also DfEE's greater role in determining these policies in collaboration with the DSS. This said, taking publication dates as indicative of acquisition dates, it would appear that the DfEE library had acquired MDRC publications long before the DSS library did or, at least, had acquired earlier MDRC research publications and evaluations, than the DSS had. But, whereas the DSS library continued to stock MDRC works published in the 1990s, our search found no such publications in the DfEE library.

---

[7] To avoid double counting, publications listed under both keywords were counted only under the keywords, under which they were listed first.

[8] In the case of a further 14 book and articles, their publication dates could not be determined.

[9] Acquisition dates could not be determined without placing unreasonable demand on the libraries' resources.

Figure 3.1   Workfare, welfare-to-work and MDRC publications

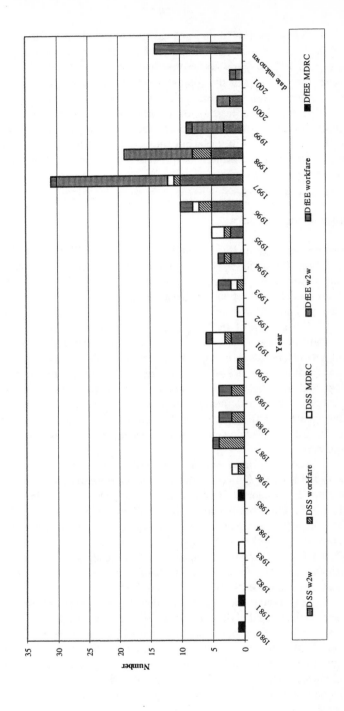

This pattern of library acquisitions matched that of the thematic focus of policy makers and analysts, who, after familiarising themselves with the findings of key (MDRC) welfare-to-work evaluations, became more concerned with the 'broader picture', that is, the context in which welfare reform took place in the US and elsewhere. Hence, an increasing number of publications would report about and reflect upon the lessons of reform programmes in other countries (e.g. Australia) or, at a more general level, discuss the implications of these lessons for the UK. The decline in the acquisition of welfare-to-work relevant publications also reflected a turn to alternative means for acquiring information. These are discussed next.

Encountering Evidence

While domestic evaluations and OECD studies still formed the backbone of information about active labour market policies that informed the design of Britain's New Deal, the use of new technology and the development of foreign contacts had already begun to impact on the way in which policy making evolved inside DSS and DfEE.

The growth of the (English-speaking) Internet facilitated policymakers' and analysts' access of information at an unprecedented scale. Policy developments reported in the media and through formal or informal overseas contacts could be quickly followed up by using electronic means to gather background information or to obtain one of the many US welfare-to-work evaluations that were appearing on the net. However, this was still not a co-ordinated effort, but one pursued by selected individuals – namely, those with access to the world-wide-web, which, in its early days, was often limited to senior civil servants.

Increasing departmental and personal contact through official channels, such as the Foreign Office's Labour Attaches reinforced this process of evidence gathering. Exploratory and exchange visits by politicians, policymakers and policy analysts, including Parliamentary Select Committees, from the UK abroad were nothing new (cp. Wolman 1992; Dolowitz 1997). Now they were playing their part in informing policy knowledge with reference to what was to become the New Deal and became important supplements to 'reading-up'. As one policymaker noted, evidence 'is as much to do with summaries of evaluation reports as it is to do with going and seeing' (Policy analyst, DSS, interviewed 14 February 2001).

Government departments organized international information conferences and seminars targeted high- and middle-level civil servants on either a regular basis (e.g. the Wilton Park conferences arranged by the Foreign Office) or one-off events. Within the then DfEE and Employment Service, policy analysts advised 'policy makers of all relevant international evidence...in other words, OECD etc., conferences, papers, as well as being steeped in and directly involved in the evaluation processes for our own programmes' (Policymaker, DfEE, interviewed 31 October 2000).

Not everyone, however, judged these conferences and seminars, or even individual visits, a success. Although the messages and lessons emanating from these events were jotted down and reports based on them were written and circulated, no formal channels existed to evaluate and digest the newly emerging information. While individuals and divisions or branches of DSS and DfEE collated some of the evidence, the absence of a central source of information gathering made the wider sharing of this knowledge difficult.

Yet, these conferences and seminars presented opportunities for subsequent follow-up meetings and, in the late 1990s, grew in importance, as policymakers increasingly looked out for policy lessons beyond their country boundaries. One important outcome of these exchanges was to increase the penetration of policy thinking by US ideas and concepts. Indeed, on occasion, welfare-to-work experts from the US took up secondments or job appointments in DfEE and the New Deal structures, including Kay Stratton, who headed the New Deal Task Force within DfEE.[10] More recently, MDRC has become the lead organization in a major evaluation of a UK labour market experiment, the Employment, Retention and Advancement Demonstration project (ERA; cp. Morris et al., 2003).

European ideas, by contrast, made few inroads on British welfare reform thinking. On the one hand, the European Union and, more precisely, the European Commission, did not have the legal competence that would have allowed the two institutions to influence welfare reform in its member states. More informal reflection about welfare reform was only just beginning to emerge from within the Commission's Employment and Social Affairs Directorate. On the other hand, with the exception of the reforms of the Dutch disability benefit system, the initiatives of individual EU member states appeared to bear few lessons for British practice, because their social security systems bore little resemblance to the British system. Thus, the scope for the transfer of policy appeared limited.

UK policymakers felt that, in the mid to late 1990s, other European countries were much less inclined to enforce stricter conditionality rules on the unemployed and other benefit claimants, than the UK. This especially seemed to be the case for countries with insurance-based social security systems. In particular, insurance-based social security systems appeared to restrict the scope for sanctioning, which was to become a key element of the New Deal (Policymaker, DfEE, interviewed 22 November 2000). From this point of view, the US evidence seemed more relevant to the UK because public assistance programmes there were built on compulsion, enforcement and sanctioning. It should be noted, however, that these programmes were mainly targeted at lone parents, who, in the UK, constituted only one of several target groups of the New Deal. Nonetheless, as will be seen, this did not stop UK policymakers from viewing the US experience with these programmes as relevant to the UK.

---

[10] Stratton had arrived in the UK after serving as Director for Employment and Training in the US state of Massachusetts.

Selecting from the Evidence

As the information gathering process gained pace, the evidence that began to emerge appeared increasingly to point in just one direction. Policy pilots and evaluations had begun to fill the evidence vacuum, but few were seen to have proven the effectiveness of specific interventions or the greater effectiveness of one type of intervention over another. This was slowly beginning to change as more and better evaluations of the outcomes of training and work experience programmes in Britain emerged. These programmes had become a major concern of policy makers and politicians as Britain's ever-fledgling training system was put under strain and threatened finally to disintegrate.

As mentioned earlier, the composition of the unemployed had become more diverse and policy needed to respond to more diverse support needs. Consequently, new small-scale policy initiatives were tried and new evaluation topics arose. Initially, these programmes and pilots were based on evidence that might have suggested that they would be effective – after all, they were trials. Ultimately, however, evidence emerged that suggested a pattern, which policy makers were quick to observe and respond to. This initial evidence was 'negative evidence' (Policymaker, DfEE, interviewed 22 November 2000), that is, it suggested traditional, undifferentiated training and work experience programmes were not effective in reducing unemployment. More specifically, they failed to integrate young people into the labour market.

This negative evidence contrasted with emerging stories from the US that a Work-First approach, which sought to move the unemployed straight into jobs rather than encourage participation in job training, *might* be effective in moving people off benefit, although the US evidence was not necessarily seen as particularly firm:

> It wasn't so much that the evidence of the effectiveness of Work-First was strong, it was more the complete absence of evidence that would support any alternative, that was what was clearly striking then (Policymaker, DfEE, interviewed 31 October 2000).

From Programmes to Approaches

At the same time as what was to be known as 'work focussed interviewing' was beginning to be seen as *'the solution'* (Policy analyst, DSS, interviewed 14 February 2001), the emphasis of policymaking shifted from 'programmes' to 'approaches'. Rather than developing and setting up programmes that were customized to the needs of variable target groups, policymakers began to develop a common set of principles, which were to guide all welfare-to-work initiatives. This approach had been harboured within the Employment Service of the DfEE and shared within the DSS, too. Within the Employment Service:

We wanted to shift the focus of the [New Deal] programme in the way in which they worked, more towards getting people into work, and put a bigger emphasis on having some service dealt with people face to face. And the role of the client advisors should become more important and they should be more ready to be approached, and that was as important if not more important than programmes (Policymaker, DfEE, interviewed 6 July 2001).

How Important was the US?

The US experience with welfare-to-work programmes was of two-fold relevance to the UK efforts to reforms its welfare and employment service programme. First, the US, through its varied array of state-led welfare-to-work programmes, provided a rich picking-ground for specific programme ideas. The main lesson taken by UK policymakers, analysts and politicians was that, for welfare reform to work, benefits payment and the provision of employment service systems would have to be moved much more closely together than had been by that time. This said, although conditionality of benefit receipt, which was at the root of such a move, was central to US welfare-to-work programmes, UK policymakers had also been made aware of its principles and practices through recent welfare reforms in Australia and the active labour market policy in Sweden (see Chapter 2).

Secondly, the specific programme idea that was identified in the US and which, in particular, New Labour politicians wanted to introduce to the UK, made the conditionality of benefits part and parcel of a grander concept that sought to promote mutual obligations between the state and its citizens and culminated in the slogan '*rights and responsibilities*'.

The fact that, at times, the US appeared to policymakers, analysts and politicians to be a supermarket full of welfare reform models may not always have worked in the US's favour. UK observers and visitors to the US have found it difficult to identify models of best practice from this vast array of initiatives that had relevance to and could be implemented in the UK. Moreover, once the focus shifted away from the large-scale and heavily promoted social experiments, such as GAIN and, more recently, Portland (Oregon), many of these programmes were judged to have lacked solid, evaluative evidence of their effectiveness:

> I think just to say generally that we were never really very convinced by any of the evidence from the US. It was always very small-scale. It always seemed very specific and very local (Policymaker, DfEE, interviewed 31 October 2000).

Others described the evaluative evidence that was available from the US at the time as 'niche evaluations' that were closer to case studies than programme evaluations (Policymaker, DfEE, interviewed 22 November 2000) and deplored programmes, which lacked 'decent evaluation, certainly any kind of comparative evaluation' (ibid.). As more evaluations were published, these fears subsided, although some UK policymakers visiting the US to study examples of best practice in welfare-to-work programmes, returned disappointed:

Well, I suppose first of all I was influenced by the One Stop shop in Madison that they were delivering out of, which was a kind of Celtic shambles as far as I can see, with no real coherence at all. And I also thought it was a deeply racist programme (Policymaker, DfEE, interviewed 22 November 2000).

Principles and Practices Observed in the US

However, policymakers' and analysts' main concern was not to import and transfer US programmes or programme details to the UK, although this did happen. Instead, it was to assess the value and effectiveness of the underlying principles of the US reforms. The single most important principle of welfare reform was quickly identified. The US experience seemed to confirm a concept that policymakers in the UK had argued for over the decade, but not managed to introduce for any long period of time: an integrated benefit and employment service system. Officials from the DSS were, above all, looking for evidence of effective alternative programme delivery mechanisms. They saw benefits in amalgamating social security and job placement services through the new front-line office position of the *personal adviser* who was an integral part of new welfare programmes in the US (as well as in Australia). This discovery of the personal adviser role would ultimately lead to the introduction of the *Intensive* or *Single Gateway* within the New Deal. In the meantime, DfEE officials also accepted the message that benefits payment should be linked to job search requirements, arguing that:

Evidence tells us that you need your active labour market policies to be fully integrated with the benefit paying system; divorce them, disaster (Policymaker, DfEE, interviewed 31 October 2000).

Because policymakers were concerned with the principles of policy delivery, the fact that the US welfare reform programmes mainly targeted lone parents, while acknowledged, did not present a major obstacle to accepting the underlying principles of welfare-to-work as observed from US examples. Policymakers believed that, in essence, US welfare-to-work programmes were succeeding because of their focus on Work-First and that, if Work-First worked for lone parents, it was also likely to work for other target groups:

One of the things I'm doing there is to oppose our unemployment insurance system with the American one, and our inactive benefit system with the American one, and come to the conclusion that the Work-First system in both...appears to be delivering the best results (Policy analyst, DfEE, interviewed 14 February 2001).

The DFEE was particularly concerned with shortening *the length of the 'dole queue'* and, for this reason, explored the role and importance of Work-First versus Human Resource Development strategies in enhancing the re-employment chances of benefit claimants. For the DSS, the policy issue posed itself somewhat differently, but only in its minutiae. The DSS was more concerned with finding ways to improve the benefit delivery system, so that the *duration of benefit claims* is shortened and also the risk of benefit fraud reduced. Conducting its search for policy ideas and new models, the DSS cast its net wider than the US by also looking to Australia and New Zealand. For both departments, the apparent solution was greater conditionality and the linking of benefit payment to active job search and, soon, the take-up of available employment or training options. It was in the US that this connection appeared most obvious:

> It was there [in Wisconsin, US] for the first time that we began to see how it was possible to bring services together and to manage them in such a way that they were both client focused, but also had this end in view of getting people...activating people and moving them closer to the labour market (Policymaker, DSS, interviewed 8 November 2000).

US Observations and UK Practice

The US also proved a good ground for observing and identifying more specific programme features, even if their implementation and the evidence base did not always impress the UK policy maker. Some of the British visitors left the US with 'a sort of series of messages about approaches that we perhaps hadn't tried enough' (Policymaker, DfEE, interviewed 31 October 2000). The key lesson concerning programme details that emerged from the US was the benefit of intensive job search and job search training. Delivering these services became the key role of the Intensive Gateway period, which is the first stage of the New Deal:

> There's been a number of things that we've done within the New Deal [that] owe quite a lot to what we saw in the United States. We introduced an Intensive Gateway, for example, that owed a great deal to the kind of intensive induction courses that we saw for welfare recipients in the States (Policymaker, DfEE, interviewed 17 January 2001).

For New Labour, the Gateway was a new concept, which DfEE pushed to be adopted as part of the New Deal. The arguments were strengthened by the fact that policymakers could not only point to US evidence, but also to similar domestic policy evidence. Between 1996 and 1997, the 1-2-1 programme, which provided individual job search advice for lone parents since 1994, had been evaluated (Boutall and Knight, 1998) and found to have been an effective instrument for helping lone parents into the labour market:

> We [DfEE] persuaded them they [New Labour] needed a Gateway on the front [of the New Deal] and we used the results of the 1-2-1 programme, which had been running under the Conservatives to demonstrate that adviser intervention would increase outflows into employment (Policymaker, DfEE, interviewed 22 November 2000).

US welfare-to-work programme evidence also appeared to suggest that there was a need to impress on clients and their personal advisers that 'Work First meant Work First, not pick a job the claimant likes' (Policymaker, DfEE, interviewed 31 October 2000). The emphasis, thus, was firmly placed on compulsion, which, at the time, distinguished the UK social agenda from that of her European counterparts, who were more reluctant to move towards greater conditionality of social security benefits and compulsion to seeking employment. Since then, of course, the experience of the Portland, Oregon welfare reform programme has suggested that, at least sometimes, waiting to pick a (good) job may, in fact, pay off. This finding has been acknowledged by some policymakers as calling for a revision of conventional perceptions of welfare-to-work programmes.

The one area that clearly distinguished the UK reform programme from the US model was the absence of time limits imposed on the receipt of social security benefits. A five-year time limit for the receipt of cash benefits had been introduced at the national level in the US in 1997 as a result of the Personal Responsibility and Work Opportunity Reconciliation Act (PRWORA). Unlike the US, for policymakers in the UK, the objective of welfare reform was not to end benefits, but to deliver a 'no-fifth option through administration' (Policy analyst, DfEE, interviewed 14 February 2001). This is a reference to the four employment and training options that are provided for under the New Deal and which indicates the mandatory nature of the programmes, which should give no room for non-participation.

The American experience, thus, served as a 'stimulus' (Policymaker, DfEE, interviewed 31 October 2000) to look again at, and appreciate the value of, the British evidence and to more firmly base the new initiative that was the New Deal on elements of programmes, which had been shown or certainly been believed to be effective in Britain. Although aspects of the American welfare-to-work experience informed the policy making process, the roots of the New Deal were equally based in the British system.

Conclusion

In his study of the introduction of the Urban Development Grant in the UK in the 1980s, which emulated the US Urban Development Action Grant, Wolman (1992, p. 42) concluded that the transfer of policy involved 'information gathering [that] is unsystematic and highly anecdotal and efforts to examine the policy effect in the original country [are] almost totally lacking'. The information gathering process that preceded the introduction of the New Deal would also have to be described as 'unsystematic'; but it was no longer 'highly anecdotal', nor were efforts to examine the policy effects in the country that served as the model for welfare reform lacking.

Information gathering was fragmented, for a long time, between different government departments, but gained greater coherence over time. As more information became available, patterns suggested by policy descriptions and policy evaluations became clearer, and awareness of welfare reform policies became more grounded in evidence. Moreover, the international evidence that emerged, in particular the US evidence, appeared to match domestic experience. With the emergence of better evidence of the effectiveness of some of these measures, both, international and domestic reform models gained greater credence.

Successive small-scale changes to, and experimentation with, social security and employment services in the UK, sometimes encouraged by the benevolent commentary of observers, such as the OECD, meant that welfare reform in the UK was a gradual process. Individual changes building on previous changes and the new structures they had evoked, welfare reform and one of its main products, the New Deal, were the outcomes of *path-dependent innovation*. They were new and innovative in so far as they introduced new administrative approaches in labour market policy and new policy principles. Yet, this process of change also depended on the coming-together of other, not unrelated developments. The New Deal came about because previous positive policy lessons derived from UK pilots (and US welfare-to-work experiments confirming these); previous legal changes, especially those entailed in the Jobseeker's Allowance Act; and because changes in the perception inside both, DSS and DfEE, of the key policy issues, all helped policy agendas to edge closer together. Most important was the conviction among policymakers that traditional, training-focussed labour market interventions would no longer succeed in an increasingly complex economy whose labour force was becoming more diverse and whose job seekers had a wide range of support needs.[11] Against this background, the New Deal was an obvious, if not inevitable, product of policy reform once agreement had been reached to modify the welfare system. Although New Labour had pushed for the early implementation of the New Deal for political reasons, the co-incidence of evidence and experience, perception and shared policy priorities greatly contributed to it.

The New Deal was, therefore, not a new departure. No radical changes or paradigmatic shift resulted. And it was not a slavish reproduction of US policy. Fortuitous circumstances, namely the election of New Labour, which replaced a Conservative Party too cautious and worried about the electoral effects of implementing reforms similar in scale and scope, produced a meeting of minds.

The emphasis that should be placed on evidence that informed the implementation and detail of policy remains difficult to estimate. Ideas were picked up en route, but because of the lack of any systematic search for ideas and evidence it is likely that other potential models of good practice were missed.

As regards the impact of US welfare reform policy on UK reforms, the answer must be that the US experience was seen to confirm UK thinking and to provide a platform that could serve to launch of the UK's *rights and responsibility* welfare model. The single major contribution of evidence from the US was its influence on the Intensive Gateway component of the New Deal, which helped to

---

[11] New Labour's readiness to invest, via the Windfall Tax, in introducing these changes also facilitated the New Deal. In fact, the previous, Conservative government's reluctance to commit to such investment may well be the main reason why Labour, not the Conservatives, produced the New Deal.

move the new welfare model away from the grand-scale job placement model dreaded by the previous Conservative government and also rejected by New Labour as too costly.

Within the civil service, however, those charged with fine-tuning the New Deal often struggled with the wealth of evidence and hearsay about the effectiveness of reform models that reached them. In the end, drawing coherent and reliable conclusions from the evidence remained difficult. This is neatly illustrated by one policymaker's commentary on the difficulties of systematically assessing a growing volume of information and evidence. The quotation presents an appropriate closure to this chapter:

> I mean it would be hard to put your finger on it, you get information from all sorts of sources, people say all sorts of things to you. This applies to ministers and to us, and that forms part of what you know and how you then react to the things that you need to put in place. So, I think it's hard to say, it would be very hard to say, here is a definite product from it, and it's had this definite effect. It would have been part of information that would have been made available to us and it would have had a marginal effect, probably. Because circumstances are different and the benefits system [in the US] is different and the culture is different and the programmes are actually different, you can't draw conclusions, which tell you what you ought to be doing. You never get anything like that. But it is just part of what of the information in place that we have (Policymaker, DfEE, interviewed 6 June 2001).

References

Boutall, S. and Knight, M.A. (1998), *Evaluation of 1-2-1 for the Very Long Term Unemployed. Tracking Study.* Employment Service RED 115. Employment Service, Sheffield.

Deacon, A. (2000), 'Learning from the US? The influence of American ideas upon "new labour" thinking on welfare reform', *Policy & Politics*, vol. 28.1, pp. 5-18.

Dolowitz, D. (1997), 'British employment policy in the 1980s: learning from the American experience', *Governance: An International Journal of Policy and Administration*, vol. 10.1, pp. 23-42.

Finn, D. (1997), Working Nation. *Welfare reform and the Australian Job Compact for the long-term unemployed.* Unemployment Unit, London.

Finn, D. (1999), 'Job Guarantees for the Unemployed: Lessons from Australian Welfare Reform', *Journal of Social Policy*, vol. 28.1, pp. 53-71.

Johnson, C. and Tonkiss, F. (2002), 'The third influence: the Blair government and Australian Labor', *Policy & Politics*, vol. 30.1, pp. 5-18.

McKay, S., Smith, A., Youngs, R., and Walker, R. (1999), *Unemployment and Jobseeking after the introduction of the Jobseeker's Allowance.* Research Report No. 99. Department for Work and Pensions, London.

Morris, S., Greenberg, D., Riccio, J., Mittra, B., Green, H., Lissenburgh, S. and Blundell, R. (2003), *Designing a Demonstration Project. An*

Employment, Retention and Advancement Demonstration for Great Britain. Government Chief Social Researcher's Office Occasional Paper Series No. 1. Cabinet Office, London.

OECD (1996), *The OECD Jobs Study: Implementing the Strategy.* OECD, Paris.

Robinson, P. (2000), 'Active labour-market policies: a case of evidence-based policy-making?', *Oxford Review of Economic Policy*, vol. 16.1, pp. 13-26.

Smith, A., Youngs, R., Ashworth, K., Mackay, S. and Walker, R. (2000), *Understanding the Impact of Jobseeker's Allowance.* Research Report No. 111. Department for Work and Pensions, London.

Weiss, C. H. with Bucuvalas, M. J. (1980), *Social Science Research and Decision-Making.* Columbia University Press, New York.

White, M. and Lakey, J. (1992), *The Restart Effect: evaluation of a labour market programme for unemployed people.* Policy Studies Institute, London.

Wolman, H. (1992), 'Understanding cross national policy transfers: The case of Britain and the US', *Governance: An International Journal of Policy and Administration*, vol. 5.1, pp. 27-45.

Chapter 4

Workfare Evaluations and Meta-Analysis

David Greenberg and Karl Ashworth

When the Omnibus Budget Reconciliation Act (OBRA) of 1981 allowed US states to vary federal welfare policies, it spawned in its wake a plethora of evaluations of welfare-to-work programmes designed to promote work and reduce welfare caseloads, the results of which were widely disseminated (Greenberg and Shroder, 1997; Walker, 1991). The evaluations measured the effects (which are usually called the 'impact') of welfare-to-work programmes on outcome indicators, such as the receipt of welfare, whether welfare recipients undertook employment, their earnings and the amount of welfare benefits they received. Some, but not all, of these evaluations also estimated the overall costs and benefits of the evaluated programmes.

Whereas the evaluations were able to gauge the effectiveness of each welfare-to-work programme for the typical welfare recipient who was assigned to the programme, they were rarely able to determine reliably the features of welfare-to-work programmes that contributed to large or small impacts—that is, to their success or failure. Social and environmental conditions affecting programme sites, for instance, were seldom taken into account. In fact, they did not need to be because the evaluation designs used by many studies, based on random assignment of welfare recipients into programme and control groups, guaranteed that programme participants and non-participants shared environmental conditions. In addition, evaluations often recorded impacts for only the first one, two, or three years after programme implementation and were thus unable to assess the long-term performance and viability of interventions. Because their evaluation period was short-term, there was again less need to control for exogenous conditions that might have affected programme impacts over time.

The quality of the evaluations is generally high, and they are often cited internationally as best practice, which other countries are seeking to emulate (Performance and Innovation Unit, 2001; Lødemel and Trickey, 2000). However, the policy learning has typically been locally specific and idiosyncratic, rather than cumulative, with programmes being designed in situ, informed only anecdotally by experience elsewhere (Greenberg, Mandell and Onstott, 2000). Moreover, a National Academy of Sciences panel recently concluded that programme evaluations had both inherent and practical limitations that permitted them to answer only a restricted set of questions (National Academy of Sciences, 2001). They cannot, for example, easily determine which kinds of programme work best in which settings and with respect to which types of client. These shortcomings in the US evaluations have rarely stopped advocates of welfare-to-work programmes in the UK, as well as in the US, from claiming their universal applicability and effectiveness.

During the mid-1990s as, one-by-one, US welfare-to-work policy evaluations became available and the results were selectively marketed in the UK, they had a marked impact on policy thinking in the UK. As discussed in Chapters 2 and 3 and elsewhere (Peck and Theodore, 2001; King and Wickham-Jones, 1999), their strongest impact was on the design of the UK's *New Deal*. The New Deal is the current flagship of active labour market policy in the UK and seeks to increase job search and employment among specific sections of the unemployed population, including younger people, the over-50s, lone parents, disabled people, and the long-term unemployed.

The US evaluation results promulgated in the UK were in most instances selected from amongst the more successful cases in the sea of experimentation in the US. A thorough understanding of the diversity of results was lacking. In fact, the growing volume of welfare-to-work experiments set in diverse circumstances made it increasingly more difficult to verify any of the prevailing claims as to the general applicability of their findings and lessons. The claims might have been accurate, but equally could have been unfounded or inflated. Nobody knew for sure.

Meta-analysis, already widely used in medical and education research, provides a means for distilling the common key findings of an amalgam of policy evaluations. Based on a comprehensive review of available evidence, meta-analysis is a check against unwarranted generalizations and unfounded myths, which can help lead to a more sophisticated understanding of the subtleties of the effects of programmes.

Research presented in the following two chapters uses meta-analysis to synthesize statistically findings from 24 random assignment evaluations of welfare-to-work programmes in the US and to explore the factors that best explain differences in performance. All the programmes included in the 24 random assignment evaluations targeted recipients of Aid to Families with Dependent Children (AFDC), which became Temporary Assistance for Needy Families (TANF) in 1996. In addition, all the programmes were mandatory (that is, non-cooperative welfare recipients could be subjected to financial sanctions by having their benefits reduced or even eliminated). The objective of the analysis was to establish the principal characteristics of welfare-to-work programmes that were associated with differences in success, distinguishing amongst variations in the services received, differences in the characteristics of those who participated in each programme, and variations in the socio-economic environment in which the programmes operated. We also examine how programme impacts change over the time from random assignment. The analysis is based on data extracted from the published evaluation reports or from official sources.

In this chapter, we discuss how the meta-analysis described in the following two chapters was conducted, the sample of 24 evaluations that were subject to the analysis, and the data extracted from these evaluations. We also identify limitations of the meta-analytic approach. Given that the unit of analysis is the programme evaluation, and that the aim is to identify which kind of programme works best in which setting, it is perhaps appropriate to coin the term 'meta-evaluation' to describe the analytic process involved.

What is Meta-Analysis?

Meta-analysis is a quantitative approach, which consists of a family of statistical techniques that are applied to synthesize findings from multiple studies (e.g. Lipsey and Wilson, 2001; Cooper and Hedges, 1994; Hunter and Schmidt, 2004). More specifically, in the context of this book, these techniques are used to synthesize findings from multiple evaluations of welfare-to-work programmes. In medicine, under the influence of the Cochrane Collaboration, a network of institutions committed to the systematic review of evidence, meta-analysis has become a corner stone of scientific advance over the last 20 years, checking trials and experiments against others so as to reverse previous incorrect conclusions that an ineffective procedure or drug is effective when it actually is not (so-called 'false positives' or Type I errors); and using the power of large numbers to identify cases in which a procedure or drug was believed ineffective when it actually is effective ('false negatives' or Type II errors). Only very recently – with the creation of the Campbell Collaboration – has a similar movement emerged in the social sciences, the lag possibly being attributable to the competing epistemological positions adopted by social science practitioners and the diversity of research methodologies used or to the fact that the wide-spread use of studies based on random assignment is a more recent phenomenon in the social sciences than in medicine.

Meta-analysis has two primary objects. The first is to provide statistically robust estimates of the size of a policy impact by pooling results across empirical studies, each of which may be based on a relatively small sample. This, in fact, is the major reason meta-analysis was initially developed and is typically the key goal in meta-analyses of conducted in medicine and psychology. Secondly, meta-analysis is used to explore characteristics that are associated with variations in the size of impacts observed in different settings and on differing occasions. Because most evaluations of welfare-to-work programmes rely on relatively large samples, it is the second goal that is the major focus of the meta-analyses of these evaluations.

Like so many other statistical techniques, the origins of meta-analysis can be traced to Karl Pearson who, in 1904, sought to pool studies to boost sample size and statistical reliability. However, meta-analysis owes its name to a psychologist, Gene Glass, who used the term in 1976 to refer to a philosophical approach, not a statistical technique. Glass argued that literature reviews should be systematic and should interpret the results of individual studies in the context of the distributions of findings. Meta-analysis extends this logic, treating study findings as the data for statistical analysis.

How is Meta-Analysis Done?

Meta-analysis relies upon the systematic accumulation of previously gathered evidence. It permits prior conclusions and assumptions to be checked on the basis of the evidence suggested by the pooled and, hence, more reliable, data and suggests new questions to be addressed. It typically involves the assembly of results from published studies, their descriptive summary, and formal regression analyses to break down the variance in the findings into that attributable to substantive concerns and that due to sampling error. The procedures can be illustrated by describing the steps we followed in conducting our meta-analysis of evaluations on welfare-to-work programmes.

Obtain estimates of programme impacts from published articles and reports It is essential that the evidence base for the meta-analysis include all studies that are relevant to the topic under investigation, hence the need for a 'systematic' review of evidence. Many proponents of meta-analysis warn of the dangers of excluding studies reporting negative findings because these are less likely find their way into publication than are those studies showing positive results (Begg, 1994). This is commonly known as the 'file drawer' phenomenon. Excluding any such studies obviously results in a biased estimate of the underlying 'true' effect and is likely to overstate the size of the impact.

We are fortunate in that the studies reported here were funded by US government agencies and reports were published irrespective of the direction of their findings, so the file drawer problem does not arise. Results from most evaluations of mandatory welfare-to-work programmes are in reports produced by the evaluators. The first step to conduct the meta-analysis described in this book was to obtain copies of these reports.

Extract information on the dependent variable In meta-analysis, the effect or impact of a programme on an outcome, which is often referred to as its 'effect size', serves as the dependent variable. In a meta-analysis of welfare-to-work programmes, the key dependent variable is the programmes' estimated impact on the earnings of participants. The estimated earnings effect might be available for a single time period (a year or a calendar quarter) or for multiple time periods. Of course, such programmes might affect other outcomes as well, including employment, welfare and unemployment compensation payments, family income, family well being (child care, school performance of children, family functioning, etc.), criminal behaviour, feelings of satisfaction, and so-forth. However, a major objective of all welfare-to-work programmes is to increase the earnings of participants. Consequently, evaluations of these programmes estimate earnings impacts more often than effects on other outcomes. However, programme impacts on employment status, welfare status, and the amount of welfare received are frequently reported as well and consequently were extracted for purposes of our study. Effects on the other outcomes listed above are also sometimes reported, but less frequently.

Extract information on the standard error of the dependent variable As discussed below, formal meta-analysis requires weighting the estimates of the programme effect size (that is, the dependent variable) by their standard errors to take into account the different precision with which the effect size estimates were obtained. If standard errors are not available from the source studies, estimates can be provided if information on the level of statistical significance of the programme effect estimate is presented. As a final source of the precision of the effect size estimate, sample sizes used to generate the effect size estimates should also be collected.

Extract information on independent variables The main purpose of meta-analyses of welfare-to-work programmes is to explain variation in estimates of programme impacts. Thus, care should be taken to collect information on the factors that may help explain cross-programme variation. In the context of a meta analysis of welfare-to-work programmes, these factors include where and when the evaluation was conducted, average client characteristics (for example, age, education, marital status, family structure, ethnicity, and pre-programme welfare and employment history[12]), measures of programme effects on the receipt of various services (for example, job search assistance, vocational training, and education), programme costs, and programme site characteristics (for example, the local unemployment and poverty rates, average income, average welfare benefits, industry and occupation characteristics, and so forth.). Although most of this information is usually available in the published evaluation reports, the site characteristics need to be extracted by the meta-analyst from other sources such as government publications and web sites.

Convert all monetary measures to current dollars This is necessary because programme evaluations have been conducted at different points in times. The conversion may be done using either the Consumer Price Index (CPI) or the Gross Domestic Product (GDP) deflator. We used the former.

Perform a descriptive analysis of the programme impact estimates After compiling all the relevant information about the evaluation studies, it is useful to display the information in a purely descriptive format. Such an analysis is presented in Chapter 5.

Perform a regression analysis to explain variation in the programme impact estimates As previously suggested the key component of a meta-analysis of welfare-to-work programmes consists of examining the independent variables that may have contributed to variation in programme impacts across the studies. The statistical method that we use to do this is regression analysis. A major advantage of estimating regressions in a meta-analysis of welfare-to-work programmes is that this allows one to isolate the effect of each independent variable on estimates of programme impacts by holding the effects of all the other independent variables constant. For example, the average education level and the racial composition of the participants in different welfare-to-work programmes may be related to one another, and each may also influence the size of programme impacts on earnings. By using regression analysis to hold racial composition constant across

---

[12] Some client characteristics (such as education and family structure) may be influenced by the welfare-to-work programme and, thus, should be measured just prior to when random assignment takes place (sometimes called the baseline period). All our measures of client characteristics pertain to the baseline period.

programmes, it is possible to isolate the effect of education level on the size of programme impacts on earnings. Similarly, by holding educational level constant across programmes, it is possible to isolate the impact of racial composition. The regression output moreover indicates the confidence that one can place in each of these two statistically estimated relationships, as well as other estimated relationships. Findings from the regression analysis are described in Chapter 6. Technical issues that arose in conducting the regression analysis are discussed in the Technical Annex that appears at the end of this chapter.

Welfare-to-Work Programmes in the US

Mandatory welfare-to-work programmes became increasingly important in the US during the 1980s, particularly after national welfare reform legislation, the Family Support Act, was passed in 1988. They are likely to be even more important in the future, though their focus and, hence, the service mix they provide will change somewhat. The Personal Responsibility and Work Opportunity Reconciliation Act (PRWORA) of 1996, which replaced the Aid to Families with Dependent Children (AFDC) programme with block grants to the states called Temporary Assistance to Needy Families (TANF), requires a substantial fraction of the caseload in each state to participate in specific work-related activities each month. Because most welfare-to-work activities count as work-related activities under PRWORA, one of the key mechanisms available to states to meet the stringent participation requirements set by the law is to increase participation in welfare-to-work programmes. Moreover, PRWORA also prohibits states from using federal block grant funds to provide cash benefits to families who have accumulated a total of five years of TANF assistance. Many policy-makers view welfare-to-work programmes as a key means of helping prepare TANF families for life without welfare.

Evaluations of the effectiveness of mandatory welfare-to-work programmes have been accumulating since the WIN demonstrations of the late 1960s.[13] Increasingly, these programmes have been evaluated through random assignment. According to Friedlander, Greenberg, and Robins (1997), the evidence seems to indicate that welfare-to-work programmes typically result in modest, but sometimes substantial, positive effects on the employment and earnings of single-parent welfare families, which are usually headed by females. The programmes are also often found to reduce the receipt of welfare and welfare payment levels of these families, but these effects are usually rather small.[14] Although the central thrust of this evidence seems fairly apparent, findings have

---

[13] The WIN (Work Incentive) programs were the first attempt to require US welfare recipients to participate in mandatory work activities. However, these requirements were only weakly enforced.

[14] The evidence is less clear for two-parent welfare families because they were studied less often. However, programme effects for these families were generally smaller than for single-parent families.

varied considerably across different evaluations (see Friedlander et al., 1997; Gueron and Pauly, 1991; Greenberg and Wiseman, 1992).

It is evident from the above that welfare-to-work programmes are often, but not always, effective, and, when they are effective, they are more effective in some instances than in others. In the absence of statistical syntheses, however, it is difficult to determine why this is the case. For policy purposes, it would obviously be useful to know whether the variation in estimates of programme effects is attributable to differences in the services that programme participants received and in how these services are delivered, differences in the attributes of the labour market they entered after leaving a welfare-to-work programme, variation in the characteristics of the participants themselves, or other factors. Meta-analysis can help provide such information. More specifically, at least in principle, it can address the following sorts of policy questions:

- Do more stringently enforced mandatory welfare-to-work programmes, as indicated by the rate at which welfare recipients are sanctioned, produce larger effects on earnings and the receipt of welfare than less stringently enforced mandatory program? Do programmes that strongly enforce mandates make enrolees better off financially? Or, do they mainly save on welfare payments through sanctions?

- Does the extent to which welfare-to-work programmes increase the services received by those assigned to them influence the magnitude of programme effects? Welfare-to-work programmes are usually not the only source for obtaining the services they provide, but they typically do increase the extent to which welfare recipients actually receive such services (Friedlander et al., 1997). Do programmes that are more effective in accomplishing this have larger effects than programmes that are less successful in increasing the receipt of services?

- Do programme effects on earnings and the receipt of welfare differ among programmes providing different combinations of services? For example, does vocational training appear to be more or less effective than remedial education or work experience?

- Do programmes that spend more per participant for a given set of services produce larger effects than programmes that spend less on the same set of services? If so, how much larger are these effects? In other words, is the greater expenditure a reasonable investment of government funds?

- Do programme effects on earnings and the receipt of welfare differ for welfare recipients with different characteristics (for example, those have worked recently versus those who have not or those who have been on the welfare rolls for a several years versus those who have short welfare histories)?

- Are programme effects on earnings and the receipt of welfare influenced by the generosity of a state's AFDC benefit levels or by local labour market conditions as indicated, for example, by unemployment rates?

- Have welfare-to-work programmes improved over time? For example, did those that operated during the 1990s have larger impacts than those run during the 1980s?
- Do programme effects on those who participated decay over time (for example, are program earnings effects smaller during the third year after being assigned to a welfare-to-work programme than during the second year)? This issue is critical for benefit-cost studies of welfare-to-work programs because such studies must make projections of how the key benefit measure, program-induced increases in earnings, will change over the work-life of former program participants. At present, there is relatively little evidence upon which to base such projections.

The Data

The meta-analysis findings presented in Chapters 5 and 6 exploit a unique database, which was assembled specifically for the purpose of addressing questions such as those appearing above. The database is maintained in Microsoft Access and presently contains detailed information on 24 evaluations of mandatory US welfare-to-work programmes, which were implemented between 1982 and 1996 in over 50 sites (see Table 4.1).[15]

To ensure comparability among the evaluation studies in the database, inclusion criteria were established relating both to the kind of programmes being evaluated and the evaluation strategy. First, all the evaluated welfare-to-work programmes had to include an active intervention (e.g. job search, work experience, education, or training) that was intended to assist welfare recipients increase their earnings and move off benefit. Secondly, all programmes were mandatory in the sense that recipients who did not participate in job-search, vocational training, remedial training or 'work experience' as required were potentially liable to sanction through the reduction or removal of their welfare benefit. Voluntary programmes were excluded from the meta-analysis because observed effects generated by these studies are much more likely than mandatory programmes to be subject to selection effects into the programme. Such selection effects could produce biased estimates of outcome impacts, unless appropriately treated (Friedlander et al., 1997).

Thirdly, all programmes were directed at persons in receipt of AFDC (Aid to Families with Dependent Children), which during this period was the major cash public assistance programme for families in the United States. The population of interest is therefore taken to be all AFDC welfare recipients, with the

---

[15] Between 1982 and 1996, changes in state AFDC programmes could not be made without first obtaining waivers from the US Department of Health and Human Services (DHHS). In most instances, DHHS required random assignment evaluations of the changes as a condition for receiving waivers. We have checked with DHHS to verify that the 24 studies listed in Table 4.1 include all the random assignment evaluations of welfare-to-work programmes that began in the US between 1982 and 1996.

Table 4.1   US welfare-to-work evaluations included in the database

Program Title	Short Programme Name	Evaluation Organization	Year of Mid-point of Random Assignment
Community Work Experience Demonstrations	West Virginia	MDRC	1983
WORK Program	Arkansas	MDRC	1983
Employment Initiatives	Baltimore	MDRC	1983
The San Diego Job Search and Work Experience Demonstration	San Diego	MDRC	1983
Employment Services Program	Virginia	MDRC	1984
Job Search and Work Experience in Cook County	Cook County	MDRC	1985
Saturation Work Initiative Model In San Diego Saturation Work Program.	SWIM	MDRC	1985
	Philadelphia	PA Department of Public Welfare	1986
Teenage Parent Demonstration	Teenage Parents	Mathematica Policy Research	1988
Wisconsin Welfare Employment Experiment	Wisconsin	University of Wisconsin	1988
California's Greater Avenues for Independence Program	GAIN	MDRC	1989
Ohio Transitions to Independence Demonstration	Ohio	Abt Associates	1990
JOBS Program	Florida	MDRC	1991

Table 4.1 continued

Program Title	Short Programme Name	Evaluation Organization	Year of Mid-point of Random Assignment
National Evaluation of Welfare-to-Work Strategies	NEWWS	MDRC	1993
To Strengthen Michigan Families	Michigan	Abt Associates	1993
The Family Transition Program	FTP (Florida)	MDRC	1994
Minnesota Family Investment Program	MFIP	MDRC	1994
Family Investment Program	Iowa	Mathematica Policy Research	1994
Vermont's Welfare Restructuring Project	Vermont	MDRC	1995
The Indiana Welfare Reform Program	Indiana	Abt Associates	1995
Jobs First	Connecticut	MDRC	1996
The Los Angeles Jobs-First GAIN Evaluation	Los Angeles	MDRC	1996
A Better Chance	ABC (Delaware)	Abt Associates	1996
Virginia Independence Program	VIEW	Mathematica Policy Research	1996

study sample drawn from this population at a given time and place. The sample population in each of the 24 studies was composed entirely or almost entirely of lone parents, well over 90 per cent of whom were female.

Finally, the meta-analysis was restricted to experimental programmes that assigned welfare recipients to treatment and control groups on a random assignment basis. Not only is random assignment considered by many to be the model or 'gold standard' of evaluation procedure, providing unbiased estimates of programme effects, this restriction effectively standardized methodological procedures. Moreover, all but two of the evaluations were conducted by just three research organizations. Each of these three organizations has over three decades of experience in implementing and monitoring random assignment procedures and each has a strong reputation for performing random assignment evaluations efficiently and effectively.

In the database, evaluation studies are first classified by evaluation, then within each evaluation by site, and then within each site by programme. For example, in the case of the recently completed National Evaluation of Welfare-to-Work Strategies (NEWWS), which was exceptionally large and complex, there is one evaluation and there are seven sites. For three of these sites, there is one programme in each; and for the remaining four sites, there are two programmes in each. Thus, there are 11 separate sets of programme impact estimates. More generally, although the data in our database was extracted from only 24 evaluations, it contains information on 64 different welfare-to-work programmes. In our analysis, we treat each programme as a separate observation.

The database is divided into five 'levels':

Level 1 lists the title of the evaluations, their evaluators, and the reports used in constructing the database.

Level 2 contains the relevant information on the sample used in each of the evaluations, including the sample sizes and the characteristics of the sample population (gender, ethnicity, age/age group, education, number of children, welfare and employment experience prior to random assignment, and so forth).

Level 3 contains both annual and quarterly estimates of several different programme outcome and impact measures, as well as their levels of statistical significance. In each instance, the gross value of the outcome for the control group and the net impact of the programme on that outcome – that is, the difference between the programme group and the control group for the outcome – were both recorded. In addition, the levels of statistical significance of the net impact estimates were recorded. These values are recorded for all the years (up to five) and all the quarters (up to 20) for which they are available.[16] Whenever the needed

---

[16] There were a few evaluations that reported program impacts on annual earnings or annual AFDC payments, but not program impacts on quarterly earnings or quarterly AFDC payments. In these instances, the annual impact estimate for the first year after random assignment was divided by four and assigned to quarter 3, the annual impact estimate for the second year after random assignment was divided by four and assigned to quarter 7, and so forth for any additional years for which the impact on earnings or the impact on welfare payments were measured.

information was available, they were recorded separately by programme site. Programme outcomes and impacts were collected for one-parent families and two-parent families separately, whenever they were available. In addition, whenever they were available, programme outcomes and impacts were recorded for both the overall programme target group and for programme sub-groups (for example, AFDC applicants and AFDC recipients, and persons with and without pre-programme job experience). The outcome and net impact measures in Level 3 include:

- Average earnings during the quarter or year;
- Percentage ever employed during the quarter or year;
- Average AFDC/TANF payment amount during the quarter or year
- Percentage ever in receipt of AFDC payments during the quarter or year;
- Net programme benefits (that is, programme benefits less programme costs) from the perspectives of participants, the government, and society as a whole.

Level 4 records programme participation statistics (for example, overall programme participation rates; programme sanction rates; and rates of participation in job search, basic education, vocational training, and work experience). Whenever it was available, this information was obtained separately for the programme group and the control group. This permits the computation of *net* participation rates—that is, the difference between the rates included for the programme and control groups. Level 4 also records the cost per participant to the government of operating each programme and indicates whether each programme tested financial incentives and time limits.

Level 5 contains socio-economic background data for each of the programme sites and for each of the evaluation years, including the local unemployment and poverty rates, the percentage of the workforce in manufacturing employment, median household income, and the maximum AFDC payment for which a family of three is eligible. Unlike the data for levels 1 through 4, which were extracted directly from the evaluation reports, the level 5 data were obtained from government sources, mainly the US Census Bureau and the US Bureau of Labor Statistics websites.

All levels of the database are linked via unique identifiers for each of the evaluations and evaluation sites and, therefore, are available for analysis. For reasons of comparability, all the financial data (including earnings, AFDC payments received, median household income, and maximum AFDC payments) have been inflated to year 2000 US dollars by using the US Consumer Price Index (CPI-U).

Not all the evaluations reported all the data items described above, and even when the desired information was available, it was often not measured or recorded in a form comparable across evaluations. As a result, the 'size' of the database varies with the type of data that are being analysed. For example, cost-benefit data are available from only 15 of the 24 evaluations. And a few evaluations, estimated impacts on earnings, but not on AFDC receive, or vice-versa, although most studies estimated both.

Limitations of Meta-Analysis for Evaluating Welfare-to-Work Programmes

The existence of different welfare-to-work programmes naturally invites comparisons. If evaluations of these different programmes exist and the findings vary, it is appropriate and informative to ask why. Unfortunately, the answers that are often provided are ad hoc and based on informal assessments. Moreover, these assessments frequently rely on a subset of available evaluations and, thus, may miss pertinent information. In contrast, meta-analysis, when done well, draws upon systematically collected evidence from all known evaluations. Subsequently, using appropriate statistical tools, it permits formal testing of hypotheses about factors that may cause variation in programme effects, while holding other factors constant.

However, while meta-analysis offers important advantages over less formal and systematic attempts to synthesize findings from welfare-to-work programme evaluations, there are often problems with the available data that create difficulties in the estimation and interpretation of the findings. Some of these limitations are intrinsic to the methodology, but (as discussed in Chapter 8) others can be potentially mitigated by changes in how evaluations of welfare-to-work programmes are conducted.

Limitations of the Available Evaluations

Meta-analyses of welfare-to-work programmes are only as good as the evaluation studies on which they are based. Unfortunately, these studies are subject to various limitations.

First, while the number of available evaluations of welfare-to-work programmes is certainly non-trivial, it is also not large. As previously indicated, we relied on findings of the effects of 64 mandatory welfare-to-work programmes. Because the number of factors that can potentially cause cross-study variation in programme effect estimations is fairly large, multicollinearity, which is caused by too many explanatory variables relative to the number of observations, is an important concern. Thus, we limit the number of explanatory variables we include in the regressions to those that we anticipate for theoretical reasons will be related to programme impacts.

Second, findings from the available evaluations may be biased for numerous reasons (Friedlander et al., 1997). However, because all the evaluations included in our database relied on random assignment, this problem should be minimized in the meta-analysis presented in Chapters 5 and 6.

Third, meta-analyses of the welfare-to-work programme itself must inevitably be based on non-experimental comparisons. One can imagine designing several different models of welfare-to-work programmes that vary in interesting ways (for example, in terms of their relative emphasis on sanctions, job search, vocational training, and so forth), drawing a representative sample of sites and randomly assigning the programme models to these sites. For political and practical reasons, however, such an approach has never been undertaken, and it is unlikely that it ever will be. Instead, the programmes that are run at a particular place and time depend on the decisions of various government bodies. Because it is difficult to control completely for the factors that influence these decisions, meta-analyses of welfare-to-work programmes are potentially subject to selection bias. Moreover, all available evaluations of welfare-to-work programmes pertain to specific sub-national geographic areas such as states, counties, or cities. In almost all instances, the sites that were evaluated are those that were willing to be evaluated. Thus, the evaluations available for meta-analysis may pertain to a non-representative set of sites.

Heterogeneity – Comparisons of Apples and Oranges

The key objective of meta-analyses of welfare-to-work programmes is to determine why programme effects vary. Thus, it is essential that variation also exist in potential explanatory variables. However, there is a possibility that the programmes included in the analysis are so different that they are essentially non-comparable. This is especially likely because, as mentioned above, the number of available sample points is limited. Thus, it is tempting to include every possible estimate of programme effects in the analysis.

Deciding exactly where to draw the line is inevitably judgmental. For example, in this book, we compare welfare-to-work programmes that emphasized training with those that stressed job search and provided relatively little actual training. In addition, some of the programmes provided financial incentives to take jobs, but most did not. Moreover, even when programmes appear similar, they may not be. For example, vocational training could last a few weeks in one programme and several months in another.

Although assessing comparability is a subjective process, Hall et al. (1994) suggest that 'if the phenomenon is conceptually broad and therefore should be demonstrated over a wide variety of contexts, then studies that vary extensively in subjects, situations, and procedures may be appropriate for inclusion'. In fact, it is important that variation exists in the types of programmes implemented between different studies in order to establish which programme components work better than others.

Measurement Problems

Another set of problems results from inconsistencies in measurement across evaluation studies. In some cases, the dependent variable is measured differently across studies. For example, earnings measures may be derived from household survey information or from official sources, such as unemployment insurance records. It is not clear that the information from these various sources is comparable (for example, survey information tends to be more inclusive because it can include earnings from those jobs that are not covered by the unemployment insurance system). In addition, the earnings may be measured over different periods of time across studies and aggregation problems may result from trying to convert the data to a consistent time period.

As indicated in the Technical Annex to this chapter, standard errors of the estimates of programme effects are required for purposes of weighting. These standard errors are not always reported in evaluation studies and adjustments have to be made using the information that is reported to provide a consistent set of standard errors across studies.[17]

There are also inconsistencies across welfare-to-work programme evaluations in the characterization of the treatment. Even more seriously, some studies do not provide enough information to characterize properly the treatment received. Differences across studies in how participation rates are measured can create problems in interpreting and comparing estimates of programme impacts. Moreover, even when participation rates are measured similarly, they may represent somewhat different phenomena. For example, 'job search' may involve several weeks of training in how to approach employers and supervised cold calls in one case and individual contacts with employers in another.

Finally, there are often problems in measuring the characteristics of the appropriate labour market. Some programme effect estimates pertain to several different labour markets, and it is not always clear how to construct an aggregate labour market measure that applies to the population being studied. In addition, some studies take place in sites that do not correspond exactly to the geographic area for which aggregate information is available in published sources.

Dependence of Observations

The regression model presented in the Technical Annex assumes that the outcomes (e.g. estimates of programme impacts) are statistically independent. In practice, however, this assumption may not hold. For instance, a single study may present impact estimates for several time periods, several different outcome measures, several programmes, and/or several subgroups (men and women, blacks and whites, high school graduates and dropouts, and so forth). For these reasons, the assumption of independence among the sample observations may be untenable.[18]

To some extent, the meta-analyst can control for such dependence by including explanatory variables for training type, calendar time, and so forth, an approach that is used in the meta-analysis described in Chapters 5 and 6. In

---

[17] Many welfare-to-work programme evaluations use asterisks to indicate whether estimated programme effects are statistically significant at the 1, 5, and 10 per cent levels or are non-significant. The method we use to deal with this limitation is described in the Technical Annex to this chapter.

[18] For discussions of statistical dependence and ways of dealing with it, see Cooper and Hedges (1994) and Lipsey and Wilson (2001).

addition, we examine each impact measure separately. Furthermore, we do not examine impact estimates for separate subgroups.

In our judgment, the most important dependence problem that arises in the meta-analyses described in this book results because most of the 24 evaluation on which it is based report impact estimates on a number of occasions after random assignment. These estimates are included in the analysis for all the calendar quarters after random assignment for which they are available. However, as indicated above, observations that pertain to different time periods are not statistically independent of one another. Thus, in addition to regressions that are pooled over all available calendar quarters, we have also produced regressions limited to impact estimates that pertain to only a single time periods—specifically, the third calendar quarter after random assignment and the seventh quarter after random assignment. Findings from these three sets of regressions are fairly similar to one another.

Summary

This chapter has described meta-analysis and pointed out some of the limitations of these methods. In addition, it outlines US efforts to conduct random assignment evaluations of mandatory welfare-to-work programmes and describes a unique database that was developed from information provided by these evaluations. The following two chapters apply the tools of meta-analysis to this database to synthesize statistically the key findings from welfare-to-work experiments conducted in the US and to explore how the services provided by the evaluated programmes the characteristics of those participating in the programmes, and features of the local environment in which they operated influenced the size of their impacts.

Technical Annex

Two types of statistical models can be used to isolate the effects of various factors that cause programme effects to vary across studies. These models are termed 'fixed effect' and 'random effects' models, although the latter is really a generalization of the former and is more appropriately termed a 'mixed effect' model.[19] Most of the meta-analysis findings reported in this book are based on the fixed effect model. However, some results that utilize that mixed effects model are also presented. Thus, we describe both models.

Both the fixed and the mixed effects models take into account the fact that the individual underlying effect estimates are based on different sample sizes and, hence, have different levels of statistical precision. It would not make sense to weigh two studies equally that produce estimates having very different levels of statistical precision. For example, suppose one study produced an estimated impact of a particular welfare-to-work programme of $5,000, but this estimate was very imprecise and not statistically significant because of a small sample size of, say, only 500 persons. Suppose another study produced an estimated effect of $1,000 for the same programme, but was very precisely estimated because of a much larger sample of, say, 4,500 persons. If we did not take the sample sizes into account, we would conclude that the average effect of the programme was $3,000 (the unweighted mean of the estimates produced by the two studies). However, the average impact is probably closer to $1,000 because of the total sample used in the two studies (5,000), 90 per cent was from the latter study.[20]

To introduce the sort of weighting that is necessary in meta-analysis, we begin by positing the following formal statistical model, which is implicitly used in Chapter 6 to explain variation in estimates of the impacts of welfare-to-work programme:

$$(1) \quad T_i = T_i^* + e_i,$$

where T_i is the estimated welfare-to-work programme impact for programme i, T_i^* is the true' welfare-to-work programme impact for programme i (obtained if the entire target population had been evaluated), and e_i is the error due to estimation on a sample smaller than the population. It is assumed that e_i has a mean of zero. The variance of the sampling error of each of the estimated welfare-to-work programme impacts, v_i, is computed as the square of the standard error of the estimate

To provide an estimate of the mean impact that takes account of the fact that v_i varies across programme effect estimates (that is, v_i is smaller for programme impact estimates that are based on larger samples), a weighted mean can be calculated, with the weight being the inverse of the v_i, $1/v_i$. If sampling variation were the only source of variation in the welfare-to-work programme impact, weighting in this manner produces the most precise estimate of the mean programme impact.

---

[19] These models are discussed in detail in Raudenbush (1994).

[20] For further discussion, see. Lipsey and Wilson 2001, Hedges 1994, and Shadish and Haddock 1994.

However, there are two other sources of variation in estimates of welfare-to-work programme impacts. One stems from various factors that can be measured – for example, the fact that the estimates are produced for different programmes, over different time periods, for different population groups, in different locations, and so forth. The other results because there are unmeasured factors that cause variation in programme impacts. These could be related to staff attitudes toward welfare-to-work programme participants and other features of the programme or environment that are unmeasured in most evaluations of welfare-to-work programmes.

All three sources of variation may be identified by extending the model described by equation (1) in the following way:

(2) $T_i^* = \beta_0 + \beta_1 X_1 + \beta_2 X_2 + \beta_3 X_3 + \ldots \beta_p X_p + u_i,$

where β_0 is the model intercept, the Xs are observed characteristics of the evaluated programmes that cause variation in the true programme effects T_i^* (e.g., differences in programme services, client characteristics, and programme environmental characteristics), the βs are coefficients representing the marginal effects of the characteristics on the true programme effect, and u_i is a random error term with variance σ^2, representing unmeasured factors causing variation in programme impacts. Equation (2) is sometimes termed a 'structural' model in the meta-analysis literature.

Together, equations (1) and (2) constitute a statistical model of the variation in programme impacts. Substituting equation (2) into equation (1) yields the mixed effect model:

(3) $T_i = \beta_0 + \beta_1 X_1 + \beta_2 X_2 + \beta_3 X_3 + \ldots \beta_p X_p + e_i + u_i.$

In equation (3), there are three potential sources of variation in T_i – sampling error (the e_i), observed characteristics of the evaluated programmes (the Xs), and random error (the u_i). If the βs are not zero, but u_i is identically zero for all studies, then the model is referred to as a 'fixed effects' model. In the fixed effect model, there are only two sources of variation in the estimated programme effects – sampling error and variation in observed characteristics of the evaluated programmes. The weight used in estimating the fixed effects model is the inverse of the sampling variance ($1/v_i$), because the only source of variation in the estimates, other than the Xs, is the sampling variance. If the βs are not zero and u_i, as well as e_i, varies across studies, then the model is referred to as a 'mixed effects' model. In the mixed effects model, all three sources of variation in the estimated programme effects occur. The weight used in estimating the mixed effects model is the inverse of the sum of the sampling error plus the random effects error ($1/[v_i + \sigma^2]$).[21] Clearly, the fixed effects model is a special case of the mixed effects model. It is possible to test statistically for the significance of the fixed and random effects.[22]

---

[21] To estimate the mixed effects model, an estimate of σ^2 is obviously needed. Raudenbush (1994) describes several procedures for estimating σ^2, including method of moments estimators and maximum likelihood estimators.

[22] In addition to the fixed and mixed effects models, there is a third model, called the "unweighted model," in which it is assumed that there is no variation in the v_i across studies.

Unfortunately, the evaluations in our database did not typically report the exact value of the variance of the program impact estimates, but instead reported that estimates of program impacts were not statistically significant or were significant at the 1 per cent, 5 per cent, or 10 per cent level. Thus, the standard errors had to be imputed in order to obtain the weights needed to estimate either the fixed effects model or the mixed effects model, except for those relatively rare instances when exact standard errors were provided. To do this, we used the following approach. First, for impacts that were significant at the 5 or 10 per cent levels, we assumed that P was distributed at the midpoint of the possible range, i.e. if $0.1 < P < 0.05$, P was assumed to equal $P = 0.075$; and if $< 0.05 < P < 0.01$, P was assumed to equal 0.03. Second, cases for which impacts were significant at the 1 per cent levels have an unbounded t-value and cases for which impacts were non-significant can have extremely small standard errors. Therefore for these cases, we used the following procedure: (1) we multiplied each of the standard errors imputed as described above for impacts that were significant at the 5 or 10 per cent levels by the square root of the sample on which the impact estimate was based; (2) we computed the average of the values derived in (1); (3) for cases in which impacts were significant at the 1 per cent level or were non-significant, we imputed the standard error by dividing the constant derived in (2) by the square root of the sample size on which the impact estimate was based.

An alternative to meta-analysis for modelling variation in welfare-to-work programme effect estimates is *multilevel* or *hierarchical analysis*. Both meta-analysis and hierarchical analysis use statistical methods to synthesize information provided by programme evaluations. However, while meta-analysis relies on programme effect estimates that are obtained from existing evaluations, hierarchical analysis utilizes both individual-level and site-level data (that is, multilevel data). In essence, the analyst simultaneously estimates programme effects on individuals and examines the factors that cause these effect estimates to vary across the evaluation sites (Bryk and Raudenbush, 1992; Kreft and De Leeuw, 1998). Hierarchical analysis ideally requires that uniform data collection methods are used across study sites, and, thus, is rarely feasible when different programmes are run in different sites, or at least should be used with great care. Consequently, there are few instances in which hierarchical analysis has been used to synthesize multiple programme evaluations. However, one such hierarchical analysis has recently been conducted for training programmes for welfare recipients (Bloom et al., 2003). Although the research described in Chapters 5 and 6 of this book relies

---

If all studies have the same sample sizes, then the unweighted model is appropriate and can be estimated by a simple ordinary least squares regression of the programme effects on the observed characteristics. The unweighted model may also be appropriate if there is uncertainty about the accuracy of the estimated standard errors from the underlying studies, and it must be used if standard errors of the programme effects are not available for the studies. An alternative to using the standard errors to weight the observations is to use the sample sizes (typically, there is a close correspondence between the standard error and the sample size).

on meta-analysis, rather than hierarchical analysis, in Chapter 6 we also briefly compare our findings with those of Bloom et al (2003).

References

Begg, C. (1994), 'Publication Bias', in H. Cooper and L.V. Hedges (eds.), *The Handbook of Research Synthesis,* Russell Sage Foundation, New York.

Bloom, H.S., Hill, C.J., and Riccio, J. (2003), 'Linking Program Implementation and Effectiveness: Lessons from a Pooled Sample of Welfare-to-Work Experiments', *Journal of Policy Analysis and Management*, Vol. 22, pp. 551-575.

Bryk, A.S. and Raudenbush, S.W. (1992), *Hierarchical Linear Models,* Sage, Newbury Park, CA.

Cooper, H. and Hedges, L.V. (eds). (1994), *The Handbook of Research Synthesis*, Russell Sage Foundation, New York.

Friedlander, D., Greenberg, D.H., and Robins, P.K. (1997), 'Evaluating Government Training Programmes for the Economically Disadvantaged', *Journal of Economic Literature*, Vol. 35, pp. 1809-1855.

Glass G. (1976), 'Primary, Secondary and Meta-Analysis of Research', *Education Research*, Vol. 5, pp. 3-8.

Greenberg, D., Mandell, M. and Onstott, M. (2000), 'The Dissemination and Utilization of Welfare-to-Work Experiments in State Policymaking', *Journal of Policy Analysis and Management*, Vol. 19.3, pp. 367-382.

Greenberg, D and Shroder, M. (1997), *Digest of Social Experiments*, Urban Institute Press, Washington, DC.

Greenberg, D. and Wiseman, M. (1992), 'What Did the OBRA Demonstrations Do?', in C.F. Manski and I. Garfinkel (eds.), *Evaluating Welfare and Training Programmes,* Harvard University Press, Cambridge, MA, pp. 25-75.

Gueron, J. M. and Pauly E. (1991), *From Welfare to Work*, Russell Sage Foundation, New York.

Hall, J.A., Tickle-Degnen, L., Rosenthal, R., And Mosteller, F. (1994), 'Hypotheses And Problems In Research Synthesis', In H. Cooper And L.V. Hedges (Eds.), *The Handbook Of Research Synthesis*, Russell Sage Foundation, New York City.

Hedges, L.V. (1994), 'Fixed Effects Models', in H. Cooper and L.V. Hedges (eds.), *The Handbook of Research Synthesis*, Russell Sage Foundation, New York.

Hunter, J.E. and Schmidt, F.L. (2004), Methods of Meta-Analysis: Correcting Error and Bias in Research Findings, Sage, Newbury Park.

King, D. and Wickham-Jones, M. (1999), 'From Clinton to Blair: The Democratic (Party) Origins of Welfare-to-Work', *The Political Quarterly*, Vol. 70.1, pp. 62-74.

Kreft, I. and De Leeuw, J. (1998), *Introducing Multilevel Modeling,* Sage, London.

Lødemel, I. and Trickey, H. (2000), 'An Offer You Can't Refuse': Workfare in an International Perspective, Policy Press, Bristol.

Lipsey, M.W. and Wilson, D.B. (2001), *Practical Meta-Analysis,* Sage, Thousand Oaks, CA.

National Academy of Sciences, National Research Council, Panel of Data and Methods for Measuring the Effects of Changes in Social Welfare Programmes (2001), *Evaluating Welfare Reform in an Era of Transition*, National Academy of Sciences, Washington, D.C.

Pearson, K. (1904), 'Report on Certain Enteric Fever Inoculation Statistics', *British Medical Journal*, Vol. 3, pp. 1243-6.

Peck, J. and Theodore, N. (2001), 'Exporting Workfare/Importing Welfare-to-Work: Exploring the Politics of Third Way Policy Transfer', *Political Geography*, Vol. 20, pp. 427-460.

Performance and Innovation Unit (2001), *Adding It Up: Improving Analysis and Modelling in Central Government*, London: Performance and Innovation Unit, Cabinet Office.

Raudenbush, S.W. (1994), 'Random Effects Models', in H. Cooper and L.V. Hedges (eds.), *The Handbook of Research Synthesis*, Russell Sage Foundation, New York.

Shadish, W.R. And. Haddock, C.K. (1994), 'Combining Estimates Of Effect Size', In H. Cooper And L.V. Hedges (Eds.), *The Handbook Of Research Synthesis*, Russell Sage Foundation, New York.

Walker, R. (1991), Thinking about Workfare: Learning from US Experience, HMSO, London.

Chapter 5

A Description of US Welfare-to-Work Programmes

Karl Ashworth and David Greenberg

Welfare-to-work programmes typically combine a variety of services and incentives, each of which is intended to help move recipients back into work and off the welfare rolls. However, in addition to these programme components, client and area characteristics may also influence the, size and direction of the effect of a welfare-to-work programme. A programme that is effective under certain conditions, or for certain types of clients, may not be effective under other conditions or for other clients. Consequently, the extent to which a particular programme would be effective in circumstances other than those in which it operated is usually not clear from an evaluation of it.

From the perspective of the policy maker, programme characteristics are typically those factors that are most amenable to policy management. As such, knowing which of these work, and for whom, and under what conditions provides crucial knowledge to aid optimal policy design. The meta-analysis reported in Chapter 6 capitalizes on the variation in programme design, client composition and area characteristics among different mandatory welfare-to-work programmes for AFDC recipients implemented between 1983 and 1996 in the US. As explained in Chapter 4, these programmes have not been deliberately designed to explore variations in these component characteristics. In fact, it is not apparent that policy makers have given much attention, if any, to client composition or the prevailing local socio-economic circumstances in designing welfare-to-work programmes. Nonetheless, variation among welfare-to-work programmes in services provided, client characteristics, and local socio-economic circumstances supplies useful information that can be exploited to learn more about how these factors affect programme outcomes.

The primary aim of this chapter is to give a general description of the welfare-to-work programmes included in our database in order to help readers better understand the analysis reported in Chapter 6. Additional detail is given on the programmes comparing their characteristics over time. However, whilst it is informative to explore the evolution of mandatory welfare-to-work programmes, understanding how programme design over time changed was not a primary aim of this study. Consequently, it is often only possible to speculate upon reasons for change, rather than to give answers based upon detailed analysis of the rationale for the design of each programme.

A brief description of the database is given in section 4.4, along with a list of primary sources. This chapter and the following one rely on information taken from the evaluation reports concerning the outcome measures and programme and participant characteristics. As noted in Chapter 4, additional data on local socio-economic measures of well-being were obtained from external sources. Outcome and local socio-economic characteristics are time varying (that is, their values change over time) and this is reflected in the measures. Programme and participant characteristics are treated as fixed over time because they were usually measured only once. Participant characteristics were measured at the time of random assignment. Programme characteristics were often measured one year after random assignment, but this varies among the evaluations.

Description of the Programmes, Participants and Sites

The welfare-to-work programmes analysed in this and the next chapter were directed at lone parent households receiving AFDC, rather than the much smaller number of programmes aimed at two-parent households in receipt of benefit. Each statistic presented in this section is based on the maximum number of evaluated programmes for which the necessary data are available.

Programme Characteristics

The various programme components that were available under the welfare-to-work programmes were grouped as follows:

- Job Search
- Vocational Training
- Basic Education
- Unpaid Work Experience
- Paid Work Experience
- Sanctions
- Participation in any programme activity

Table 5.1 indicates the percentage of welfare recipients who were randomly assigned to a programme group that took part in each programme component. However, it is not known if, in any given programme, a particular service offered to individuals in the programme group was superior to the corresponding service offered to members of the control group. Similarly, there may well be variation in the quality of a particular service offered to welfare recipients by different programmes, but again it has not been possible to identify and code for any such difference.

Table 5.1   **Average participation and sanction rates of US welfare-to-work programmes**

(in %)

	Gross	Net
Participation in any	54.1	22.6
programme activity	(12.7)	(12.0)
Job Search	30.7	21.5
	(14.7)	(12.4)
Vocational Training	20.3	3.6
	(11.3)	(4.7)
Basic Education	16.5	7.0
	(11.3)	(10.6)
Unpaid Work Experience	6.1	3.0
	(5.9)	(5.2)
Paid Work Experience	3.3	0.4
	(3.2)	(1.5)
Sanctions	12.5	8.0
	(13.1)	(10.0)
N	51	50

Note: data averaged over programmes with valid impact data at the third quarter after random assignment. N is the maximum number of valid values. Due to missing values, some of the figures in the table are based on fewer observations. Standard deviations in ( ).

A participant assigned to a programme group did not necessarily receive any of the programme's services. Indeed, across all 51 evaluation sites for which the data are available, only around half (54.1 per cent[23]) of the persons randomly assigned to a programme group took part, on average, in any activity (Table 5.1, 'gross' column). Non-participation could have arisen for a number of reasons. For example, recipients might have left benefit before they became eligible for any of the programme services, or they may have been excluded from participation (e.g. because of illness). Alternatively, a recipient could have refused to participate, in which case they became at risk to the enforcement of sanctions; or they could have simply fallen through cracks in the system because of a failure to enforce the participation sanction.

Job search was the most common programme activity, on average, undertaken by just under one-third (31 per cent) of individuals assigned to the

---

[23] This figure, as well as others in this chapter, applies an equal weight to all programme observations, rather than adjusting for the programme's sample size relative to the overall pooled sample size. Whilst this procedure is not strictly correct, it provides a clearer picture of the data as they are used for explanatory purposes in the regression models described in Chapter 6.

experimental group. Overall, an average of 20 per cent of programme participants undertook vocational training and 17 per cent engaged in basic education. In many instances, participants were able to join both types of courses simultaneously or sequentially. Markedly fewer participants undertook work experience. This was particularly true for paid work experience, which on average was undertaken by only three per cent of programme participants. Almost twice as many took part in unpaid work experience, but this still amounted to an average of only six per cent of all programme participants. On average, 13 per cent of programme participants were sanctioned for violating programme rules. These sanctions typically either reduced or eliminated their welfare grant for a period of several months.

The gross participation rates suggest that welfare-to-work programmes typically provide both labour market attachment activities (through job search) and human resource development (through training activities). Net participation rates take account of the percentage of individuals in the control group who took part in similar activities that were provided outside the evaluated programmes. The net participation rates demonstrate that the programmes being evaluated typically put much more emphasis on increasing participation in relatively inexpensive work-first activities, such as job search, than on increasing participation in human resource development activities, such as basic education and vocational training.

Overall, the welfare-to-work programmes increased net participation by an average of 23 percentage points (a rise of around 42 per cent). Only around one-third (31.5 per cent[24]) of the control recipients who were not assigned to an experimental regime routinely participated in a welfare-to-work activity as a part of their welfare experience. The mandatory nature of these programmes, exemplified by the eight-percentage point net increase in sanctions, probably contributed to this rise in programme participation.

The singularly greatest contribution of the evaluated welfare-to-work programmes was to increase participation in job search activities by 22 percentage points. The programmes' net contributions to other activities, including those aimed at promoting human resource development, were considerably smaller; participation in basic education increased by just seven percentage points and participation in vocational training by less than four percentage points. Indeed, in some individual programmes with a work-first emphasis, participation in these activities and in work experience actually declined.

Changes in Participation Patterns over Time

Turning next to the evolution of welfare-to-work programmes, it appears that the concept of actively helping people off benefit gained in credibility over time. As suggested by Table 5.2, welfare recipients who were assigned to the control group were increasingly likely to participate routinely in an activity. For example, in programmes implemented between 1982 and 1989, control group participation in some activity was at 19.3 per cent, rising to 34.3 per cent in programmes beginning

---

[24] Control group level of participation equals gross participation minus net participation.

operations between 1990 and 1993, and reaching 38.9 per cent in programmes introduced between 1994 and 1996.

Table 5.2   Activity participation rates over time of US welfare-to-work programmes

(in %)

	1982-1989	1990-1993	1994-1996
Gross participation	51.5	57.3	52.7
	(12.7)	(9.2))	(16.8)
Net participation	32.2	23.0	13.8
	(15.0)	(8.3)	(7.0)
Gross sanction	10.9	11.0	17.8
	(14.2)	(11.0)	(14.6)
Net sanction	7.6	6.6	10.8
	(9.4)	(7.4)	(14.3)
Gross job search	28.8	30.1	34.0
	(17.1)	(14.2)	(12.1)
Net job search	27.5	19.8	16.0
	(15.1)	(9.1)	(9.9)
Gross basic education	18.6	18.0	11.1
	(15.2)	(10.1)	(5.2)
Net basic education	10.5	7.5	1.4
	(12.7)	(10.7)	(3.2)
Gross vocational training	17.6	24.6	15.8
	(11.6)	(9.6)	(12.0)
Net vocational training	3.0	5.4	1.6
	(3.2)	(5.2)	(4.9)
Gross paid work experience	0.8	4.2	5.4
	(1.4)	(3.1)	(3.7)
Net paid work experience	0.1	0.4	0.7
	(0.8)	(1.6)	(1.9)
Gross unpaid work experience	6.7	5.9	5.5
	(8.3)	(4.2)	(3.4)
Net unpaid work experience	5.0	1.7	2.1
	(7.9)	(2.4)	(2.6)
N	18	20	12

Note: evaluated using data averaged over sites with valid data at quarter 3 (N is the maximum and varies across variables because of missing values).

Perhaps surprisingly, net participation declined over the same time periods from 32.2 per cent in the 1983-89 period to 23 per cent in the 1990-93 period and 13.8 per cent in the 1994-96 period. Consequently, gross participation was the same in the third time period as it was in the first (52-3 per cent), although it peaked in the second period (57.3 per cent).

This study was not designed to explore the reasons behind the trends in the evolution of welfare-to-work programmes, so it is only possible to speculate about why gross participation remained fairly constant. It should also be borne in mind that the time at which the measures of participation were taken typically occurred comparatively soon after random assignment. Thus they may not indicate the percentage of individuals who ever participated in a programme activity while on the AFDC rolls.

One potential set of explanations for the lack of increase in gross participation rates over time relates to resource-based constraints. Benefit staff can only see a certain number of people in a given time period. The data in Table 5.2 suggest that welfare officers were routinely seeing more control group, members in more recent years than in earlier years. Consequently, unless staff numbers were increased sufficiently, this would limit available staff time with programme group recipients. Hence, the overall proportion of recipients in the combined control and experimental groups allocated to programme activity would be expected to remain approximately constant.

Another reason is that some of the more recent programmes in our sample emphasize financial incentives and (to a lesser extent) time limits. As a result, these programmes may have put less emphasis than earlier ones on increasing service receipt among experimentals. It is also possible that there is a natural ceiling to gross participation rate that is less than 100 per cent. Consequently, as the participation rate for controls increases, the net rate must fall.

It is informative to examine the evolution of work-first and human capital approaches over time, as evidenced by the extent to which programmes implemented at progressively later calendar dates included those activities that are associated with each approach.

Help with job search was made available early on in welfare-to-work programme designs, with 28.8 per cent of experimental programme recipients in programmes implemented between 1982 and 1989 receiving some sort of help with their job search. However, help with job search was new, as only 1.5 per cent of controls received help with job search during this period. However, it gained in popularity. Comparing programmes starting in 1982-1989 to those starting in 1994-1996, gross job search rates increased over time from 28.8 per cent to 34 per cent. In addition, it became a staple component of routine welfare provision. Net job search declined from 27.5 per cent in programmes implemented between 1982 and 1989 to 16 per cent in programmes undertaken between 1994 and 1996. Conversely, routine provision, for controls, rose from the 1.5 per cent observed in the 1982-1989 period to 18 per cent in the most recent period (1994-1996).

Accompanying the work-first approach adoption of job search was an increasing use of sanctions. Sanctions increased both among experimental group and control group recipients. Sanctions became increasingly likely to be applied routinely and their application was even more likely to become a part of an experimental programme. In 1982-1989 gross sanction rates were 10.9 per cent, which along with a net sanction rate of 7.6 per cent indicates that few control group members were sanctioned (3.5 per cent). By 1993-1996, gross sanction rates had increased to 17.8 per cent, on average, net sanction rates to 10.8 per cent and control group rates to seven per cent.

Vocational training (14.6 per cent) and basic education (8.1 per cent) were infrequently routinely on offer for controls in the 1982-1989 period. Moreover, the use of vocational training was not much expanded by the experimental programmes, with a net participation rate of just three per cent and thus a gross rate of 17.6 per cent. Vocational training became more popular in the 1990-1993 period with a gross participation rate of 24.6 per cent, but the net rate was still only 5.4 per cent. Vocational training then lost ground in the 1994-1996 period, with gross participation dropping to 15.8 per cent. Although 14.2 per cent still routinely received it in the control group, the net rate was only 1.6 per cent.

The use of basic education was much more likely to be expanded by the evaluated welfare-to-work programmes in our sample than was vocational training. In the 1982-1989 period, 18.6 per cent of the experimental group received basic education compared to 8.1 per cent of the control group. Thus, the net rate was 10.5 per cent. In the 1990-1993 period, basic education appeared to remain an integral part of experimental policy planning, with a gross rate of 18 per cent and a net rate of 7.5 per cent. However, it apparently fell out of favour between 1993 and 1996, with the gross rate falling to 11.1 per cent and the net rate to 1.4 per cent.

Work experience played little part in routine or experimental programme activities. Paid work experience was hardly apparent at all in the 1982-1989 period with a gross participation rate of less than one per cent. During the 1990s, between 4-5 per cent of those assigned to the programme group received some paid work experience, but net participation rates were less than one per cent. Unpaid work experience was more prevalent than paid work experience in the 1982-1989 period, with 6.7 per cent of the experimental group receiving unpaid work experience. The net participation rate was comparatively high at five per cent. The gross participation rate for unpaid work experience decreased slightly during the 1990s, and the net rate decreased markedly.

In summary, it is clear that the experimentally tested welfare-to-work programmes mainly relied on increasing the use of sanctions, job search and basic education over their routine use as exemplified by participation rates among controls. However, net participation rates in job search and (especially) basic education fell substantially between the 1980s and the 1990s.

Characteristics of Programme Participants and Socio-Economic Conditions

As shown in Table 5.3, women formed the vast majority of AFDC participants in lone parent families who were randomly assigned in a typical welfare-to-work programme (93 per cent). This is unsurprising given that females head most lone parent households in the US. On average, 45 per cent of participants were black, 39 per cent were white and most of the remainder were Hispanic. However, welfare caseloads in some of the evaluation sites were almost exclusively white and in others largely black (as indicated by the large standard deviations).

Table 5.3   Characteristics of US welfare-to-work programme participants and sites

Participant Characteristics	%	Area Socio-Economic Conditions	% / $
Female	92.9	Unemployment rate	6.6
	(5.7)		(2.6)
Black	45.3	Poverty rate	14.7
	(24.5)		(4.8)
White	38.6	Workforce in	11.80
	(23.1)	manufacturing employment (%)	(4.75)
Sites with average age of participants under 30	39.1 (49.3)	Maximum AFDC payment for a family of 3($)	546.1 (201.5)
With High School degree or diploma	50.9 (8.6)	Median household income ($)	39753 (6888)
Employed in year before random assignment	43.4 (15.0)		
N	48		50

Note: Computed using data averaged over programme sites with valid data at the third quarter after random assignment. N is the maximum number of valid values. Because of missing values, some of the figures in the table are based on fewer observations. Standard deviations in ( ).

In 39 per cent of the programme sites, the average participant was aged under 30, but the high standard deviation reveals a concentration of sites with predominantly 'old' or predominantly 'young' participants. Fifty one per cent of AFDC recipients in the studies had obtained at least a high school degree or diploma, and this varied little across the evaluation sites. Finally, 43 per cent had been employed during the year before receiving AFDC, with some variation among sites.

Information on unemployment and poverty prevailing across the programme sites is available on an annual basis and is reported here for the first year after the mid-point of random assignment. Unemployment rates, which serve as indicators of the availability of work and local competition for jobs, averaged 6.6 per cent but varied considerably among the evaluation sites, as indicated by a standard deviation of 2.6. Poverty rates, which are indicative of a range of factors reflecting both individual characteristics (e.g. lone parenthood and lower educational attainment) and area characteristics (poor job availability and low wage jobs, low commercial investment, and greater segregation), averaged 14.7 per cent (standard deviation 4.8). Manufacturing employment, on average, accounted for nearly 12 per cent of total employment at the programme sites.

The mean value of the maximum monthly AFDC payment available to single parent households with two children was $546 in year 2000 dollars. The standard deviation of $202 confirms the considerable state-to-state variation in the US in the generosity of welfare systems. Median household income at the programme sites averaged nearly $40,000 (in year 2000 dollars), which translates into an average weekly income of $764.

Impact Measures: Earnings and AFDC Receipt

Unweighted quarterly data show positive programme impacts on the earnings of programme participants (Figure 5.1) and reductions in their receipt of AFDC (Figure 5.2). In both instances, impacts were measured as differences between averages for the programme participant group and the control group of non-participants during the quarters after random assignment. In the case of earnings, impacts measured a 'positive change' – that is, the average earnings of members of the programme groups less the average earnings of members of the control group. In the case of AFDC receipt, however, the impacts measured a 'negative change'. That is, a positive value indicates that fewer members of the programme group than control group receive AFDC after random assignment. The actual value indicates the percentage point difference between the two groups.

As shown in Figure 5.1, most of the earnings impacts were positive. Across all time points and evaluations, participants' earnings increased by an average of $89 per quarter (standard deviation $114). As discussed in greater detail in the following chapter, the quarterly earnings impacts increased for about three years, after which they declined. However, some caution is advised when interpreting this result. First, the number of data points decreased markedly at around this time. Thus, the sample composition in the early and later quarters differed markedly. Secondly, it is likely that studies that covered longer periods were those that reported greater early impacts; if so, this would tend to make the earnings impacts appear to have lasted longer than they actually did (Greenberg et al., 2003a).[25]

---

[25] In an analysis that is not reported here, we examined changes in earnings impacts between adjacent quarters for the same studies. Three-hundred-and-seventy-one such pair-wise

Figure 5.1   The impact on earnings over time ($, Year 2000)

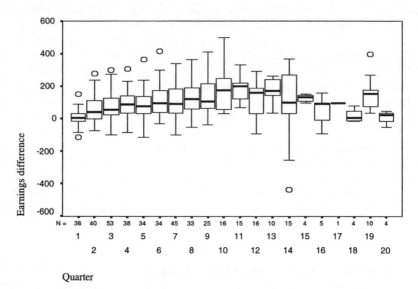

Quarter

Note: Earnings difference is measured in US dollars adjusted to year 2000 (prices). The dark horizontal bar within the box represents the median value and the interquartile range (IQR) determines the length of the box. Outlying values (O) outside of the IQR are individually plotted.

    Programme impacts were also widely dispersed. The length of the boxes in Figure 5.1, which represents the inter-quartile range (IQR), shows the general extent of this dispersion in each quarter. Thus, the longer the box, the greater the difference is between programmes at the 25th and 75th percentile of the distribution in terms of their measured impacts. In addition to the box size, the 'whisker' of the plot (the vertical bar topped by a perpendicular horizontal bar) shows the value that is 1.5 times the IQR. Values falling outside of the horizontal bars are individually printed. Values between 1.5 and 3 times the IQR in magnitude are known as 'outside values' and those over 3 times the IQR as 'extreme values'.
    In quarters two through to six, the Riverside site of California's GAIN programme appears as an 'outside value' in the box plots, exhibiting considerably higher average earnings impacts (Figure 5.1). Riverside, which placed much greater emphasis on a work-first approaches than other GAIN sites, has been much cited on both sides of the Atlantic as evidence of the effectiveness of the 'work-first' approach (Peck and Theodore, 2001). As discussed in Chapter 6, this is only

---

comparisons were made. The results, which are less subject to the sort of compositional bias discussed in the text, imply a similar quadratic relation to the one reported in Table 4, but programme impacts last slightly less long.

a part of the explanation for the exceptional nature of Riverside's success. The Lynchburg site in the Virginia Independence Programme (VIEW) appears as a high outside value in the first quarter and the Butte, California, site in the GAIN programme appears as a high outside value in quarter 19. Low outside values occurred in the first quarter in the Teenage Parent Demonstration Programme's Camden site and in the 14th quarter in the Newport site of Vermont's Welfare Restructuring Project.

Outside values were also apparent in the case of programme impacts on AFDC receipt (Figure 5.2). The impacts include a number of extreme lows with a negative difference – that is, higher AFDC receipt among members of the programme group than among control group members. Negative impacts were especially prominent in the case of Minnesota's Family Investment Programme (MFIP) and, as suggested in the following chapter, probably result because this programme provided financial incentives as well as job search and training services. A smaller number of positive outside values can also be observed in Figure 5.2, including the National Evaluation of Welfare-to-Work Strategies (NEWWS) site in Portland, Oregon in the 5th and 6th quarters. The overall mean impact on the receipt of AFDC was 1.7 percentage points, averaged across evaluations and over time (standard deviation: 3.9 percentage points). Thus, a typical experimentally evaluated welfare-to-work programme had a very modest influence in moving AFDC recipients off the welfare rolls, although some programmes had a considerably larger effect. Similar to earnings, average programme impact on AFDC receipt peaked at around the 13th quarter, after which it declined.

In summary, the initial examination of the earnings and AFDC impact measures reveals:

- Positive, but quite modest, programme impacts on earnings and AFDC receipt;
- A general upward trend in impacts for around three years, after which they declined; and
- A wide variation in both earnings and benefit receipt impacts.

Some of this variation is almost certainly due to differences in the evaluated programmes, but some may also be due to differences among the population groups studied, the time periods covered, and socio-economic conditions in the sites in which the programmes were located. The statistical analysis that is described in the following chapter examines the relative importance of these observed sources of variation.

Figure 5.2   The impact on AFDC receipt over time

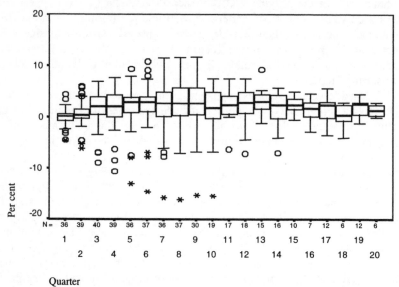

Quarter

Note: The impact is calculated as the percentage of original AFDC recipients in the evaluation in the control group who received AFDC at some time in each quarter minus the corresponding percentage for the experimental group. A positive score indicates a reduction in the AFDC caseload. The dark horizontal bar within the box represents the median value and the interquartile range (IQR) determines the length of the box. Outside values, between 1.5 and 3 times the IQR, are individually plotted as 'O', and extreme values, at over 3 times the IQR, are individually plotted as '*'

References

Greenberg, D., Michalopoulos, C. and Robins, P.K. (2003), 'A Meta-Analysis of Government Sponsored Training Programs', *Industrial & Labor Relations Review*, vol. 57.1, pp. 31-53.

Peck, J. and Theodore, N. (2001), 'Exporting Workfare/Importing Welfare-to-Work: Exploring the Politics of Third Way Policy Transfer', *Political Geography*, Vol. 20, pp. 427-460.

Chapter 6

Determining What Works
and For How Long

Robert Walker and David Greenberg

Chapter 5 dispelled the myth that workfare, making recipients work for benefit, is the only policy response that the United States has to offer to challenges faced by modern social assistance systems. While it is true that the obligations imposed on welfare beneficiaries increased during the 1980s and 1990s, especially after passage of the Personal Responsibility and Work Opportunity Reconciliation Act in 1996, states experimented with a diverse range of approaches spanning heavy investment in education and training through to work-first approaches. This diversity, combined with experimentation, is important because it offers the policymaker a smorgasbord of tried and tested options. The added attraction of meta-analysis is that it allows one to explore which components of a chosen strategy are most important in generating the desired result and to investigate whether specific approaches work best in particular settings.

As explained in Chapter 1, there is now a large measure of consensus about the importance of paid employment as a defence against poverty and social exclusion and as a route out of continued reliance on welfare benefits. However, agreement on the centrality of work has been offset by continuing debate about how best to promote success in employment. Some have argued that providing welfare recipients with skills and training that they lack, *human capital investment*, is a productive long-term strategy. This view held sway in the US in the 1980s (Walker, 1991) and underlies many of the activation schemes found in Western Europe (Lødemel and Trickey, 2001). It is also apparent in the emphasis given to accredited training in Britain's New Deal for the Young People. The countervailing position is that welfare recipients benefit most from work experience; a view neatly summarized by the dictum 'any job is better than no job'. The exceptional results observed Riverside County, California, discussed in Chapter 5 and again below, provided a sustained stimulus to the 'work-first' perspective that came to shape welfare reform in the United States in the mid 1990s. In Britain, the influence of work-first thinking is perhaps most evident in New Deal for Lone Parents which, although voluntary, focuses on engaging lone parents with the prospect of work more than on encouraging them to acquire additional qualifications.

These different approaches lend themselves to contrasting ideological interpretations. Indeed, as suggested in Chapter 1, they once provided a litmus test of conservative and liberal opinion in the United States. While meta-analysis offers a unique means of objectively testing the social effectiveness of these different ideological positions (at least in the context of welfare-to-work policy), it also advances the debate by directing attention to various neglected factors that may well have a profound influence on the effectiveness of individual policies. While it is perhaps obvious that the success of a particular policy strategy is likely to be dependent on local influences – differences, for example, in welfare caseloads, labour market conditions and implementation procedures – attention is rarely given to such matters. This neglect is partly because the impact of such influences generally cannot be deduced from one-off pilots or experiments located in comparatively homogeneous communities in which evaluators and policy administrators strive to achieve uniform implementation. By pooling all the mandatory welfare-to-work experiments it is possible to investigate the impact of environmental factors although it is impossible on the basis of the published reports to investigate the role of local leadership and management (Bloom et al., 2003; Mead, 2004).

The remainder of this chapter is divided into three parts. The first is devoted to disentangling the impact of welfare-to-work policies and seeking to deduce what portion of the observed effect is due to policy design and what is attributable to other factors. The second part focuses on two successful and very influential implementations, the one in Riverside County mentioned above, and the Portland (Oregon) Welfare-to-Work Programme; the question of import is how much of their success stems from the unique nature of the policies implemented and how much to factors beyond the direct control of administrators. A secondary question is what chance there would be of attaining similar levels of success if the Riverside or Portland models were to be implemented elsewhere. In the final section, attention turns to issue of the durability of programme impacts: are programmes effective in the long term? Is people's behaviour changed by welfare-to-work programmes and their living standards improved for years to come, or is the impact, however large, merely transient?

Explaining the Impact of Welfare-to-Work Programmes

The principles underlying meta-analysis are presented in Chapter 4 and will not be repeated here save to say that most of the findings derive from the application of a special kind of multiple regression model (a pooled weighted regression model). The dependent variable, the phenomenon to be 'explained', is one of two outcomes or measures of the effectiveness of welfare-to-work programmes: either the effect on wage income or the impact on levels of welfare receipt. In each case, the measure of effectiveness is derived by comparing outcomes for two identical groups of people: one randomly chosen to receive a new welfare programme; the other randomly assigned not to receive the new programme but only to participate in pre-existing programmes. The random assignment means that the two groups are likely to be identical in all respects except participation in the new programme.

The analysis pools outcomes for all mandatory welfare-to-work experiments conducted in the US between 1982 and 1996 and all measures of outcomes recorded over the life of each programme, a total of around 440 observations. This enables local conditions to be taken into account, as well as the characteristics of all the different programmes, as so-called 'independent variables' – that is, as explanations for variations in programme effectiveness. The regression analyses are weighted to give priority to evaluations that generated the most precise measures of outcome and to accord less priority to outcomes based on small sample sizes or that for other reasons may be considered less reliable.

Impact on Earnings

The first measure of effectiveness to be considered is the extent to which a programme increased the average earnings of participants compared with those of people assigned to the control group (Table 6.1). The greater the increase, the more effective the programme is judged to be. It should be borne in mind that, because judgments are being made based on averages, not everybody participating in a successful programme necessarily experienced an increase in income. Similarly, not everyone in the most successful programme enjoyed higher wage income than everybody in the second most successful programme. Moreover, it is possible that one programme could have attained the same average impact as another by securing very high incomes for a small percentage of participants while the other achieved smaller increases but for a larger proportion of participants. In this last instance, although the average increase would be the same for the two programmes, the modelling would give greater weight to the programme that achieved the more uniform, across the board increase in wage income. Finally, it should be noted that the analysis does not distinguish between people working long hours at low rates of pay and other people working fewer hours, but at higher wages.

As noted in Chapter 5, the impact of welfare-to-work programmes was generally modest at the individual level even if they proved clearly cost effective in rigorous cost benefit analyses. Taken overall, welfare-to-work programmes succeeded in raising earnings on average by $98 per quarter, or 13 per cent more that controls. However, programme-to-programme variation was very marked and differed according to when earnings gains were measured. What the analysis reveals is that these differences are not only directly attributable to characteristics of the various policy models, but also to variations in the characteristics of caseloads and differences in the buoyancy of local labour markets.

To take programme characteristics first, the results speak directly to the debate between protagonists of human capital investment and those advocating work-first strategies. Whereas programmes emphasising job-search and sanctions were associated with above average increases in earnings, those prioritising vocational training were characterized by below average earnings. These effects were substantial compared with other factors and highly statistically significant. Measured over three months, a one percentage point increase in the proportion of participants sanctioned in a programme compared to the control translated into a

Table 6.1 **Regression model of impacts on earnings and AFDC receipt (weighted/all quarters)**

	Earnings		Receipt of AFDC	
CONSTANT	-103.63 (22.89)	***	19.439 (1.956)	***
PROGRAMME EFFECT ON % RECEIVING				
Sanctions	4.01 (.4)	***	0.102 (.01)	***
Job Search	2.66 (.36)	***	0.069 (.008)	***
Basic Education	-0.06 (.32)		-0.001 (.008)	
Vocational Training	-6.80 (.87)	***	0.160 (.023)	***
Work Experience	0.71 (.77)		-0.061 (.018)	***
PROGRAMME INCLUDES				
Financial Incentives			-8.637 (.307)	***
Time Limit			3.259 (.396)	***
PARTICIPANT CHARACTERISTICS				
% Non-White/Non-Black			-0.091 (.009)	***
% Black			-0.050 (.005)	***
% White	1.38 (.18)	***		
% Female			-0.153 (.019)	***
% with Recent Employment			-0.067 (.007)	***
Young Target Population = 1	-72.71 (7.9)	***		
SITE CHARACTERISTICS				
Maximum AFDC Payment			-0.003 (.001)	***
Poverty Rate	2.37 (.94)	**	-0.104 (.022)	***
Unemployment Rate	-3.70 (1.44)	**		
TIME				
Year of R.A. - 1982			0.225 (.03)	***
Quarters since R.A.	24.63 (2.21)	***	0.801 (.051)	***
Sq. of Quarters since R.A.	-1.12 (.13)	***	-0.035 (.002)	***
Number of Observations	438		442	

Notes: R.A. = Random Assignment. Standard errors in parentheses.
*** Significant at the 1 per cent level, ** Significant at the 5 per cent level, * Significant at the 10 per cent level.

$4.01 increase in earnings (in 2000 dollars). Similarly, a percentage point increase in net participation in job-search activities raised earnings by $2.66 compared to individuals in the control groups.

In contrast, programmes that prioritized vocational training did less well at increasing average earnings. The earnings differential between programme members and controls fell by $6.80 for each percentage point increase in the number participating in vocational training. Of course, this is to be expected shortly after joining a programme because people undertaking training have less time to work and less inclination to seek work until they have secured certification. Certainly, further analysis (Appendix 6A) indicates that the deflating effect of training on earnings outcomes was more marked in the third quarter following random assignment than in the seventh. Even so, there is no indication that programmes that emphasized vocational training were ever more successful in increasing earnings than programmes that did not. On balance, therefore, work-first programmes proved more effective at increasing earnings than those that prioritized investment in human capital.[26]

The impacts attributable to programme characteristics were assessed after taking account of labour market conditions. But, as signalled above, certain features of local labour markets in turn influenced the overall effectiveness of welfare-to-work programmes. Two characteristics were considered: the poverty rate, assessed using the official US poverty line (an absolute measure that, in 2003, equalled $14,824 or over £8,000 for a lone mother with two children); and the unemployment rate. Both the unemployment rate and the poverty rate were measured in each quarter for which assessments of programme outcomes were available. As might be anticipated, welfare-to-work strategies worked least well in regions of high unemployment and low labour demand: earnings of programme participants rose relative to those of controls by $3.70 per quarter for each percentage point fall in the local unemployment rate.[27] On the other hand, programmes located in areas characterized by extensive poverty perform relatively well: the impact on earnings increased by $2.37 for each percentage point increase in the local poverty rate. The mediating effects of unemployment and poverty on the performance of programme interventions are each case measured net of the effect of other factors; thus the constraining influence of unemployment cited above discounts any effect of, say, variations in poverty rates.

---

[26] Some additional light is thrown on this topic by a separate statistical synthesis of 18 welfare-to-work programmes by Bloom et al. (2003), which is mentioned in the technical annex to Chapter 4. They found that programme effects on earnings are larger when there is a stronger focus on quick employment, a finding that is obviously supportive of the work-first approach. In addition, their findings indicated programme earnings effects increase when the staff responsible for operating the programmes has smaller caseloads and provides more personalized attention to participants.

[27] Bloom et al. (2003) also found that the effects of welfare-to-work programmes on earnings tended to be larger in sites with lower unemployment rates.

More complex modelling (reproduced as Annex 6.1-6.3) provides a hint at the underlying mechanisms by which labour market characteristics serve to mediate the impact of welfare-to-work policies. This reveals that the negative impact of unemployment increased from the third to the seventh quarter after people were randomly assigned as participants and controls, such that by the latter time each percentage point increase in unemployment reduced the effect of programmes by about $10 per quarter. This suggests that similar proportions will gain employment or otherwise increase their earnings soon after joining a programme irrespective of local labour market conditions. Such people are either work-ready or work shy and stimulated into action by their initial involvement in a programme. Thereafter, there are two possibilities that are consistent with the findings and both may be true. First, people more distant from the labour market or with few characteristics that make them attractive to employers eventually find work or increase their earnings in buoyant economies but not in places where jobs are scarce and they remain towards the back of the job queue. Secondly, people in areas of slack demand for labour may only find temporary or dead-end work that prevents them from enjoying a growth in earnings attributable to employment progression and/or work experience and enhanced skills.

The modelling indicates that the mediating influence of poverty declines over time but also that welfare-to-work policies work better in areas of comparative prosperity or great deprivation than in districts with average poverty rates. (This is indicated by the significance of a quadratic term in the regression equation, Annex 6.1) Programmes may be particularly effective in areas of acute poverty because they engender hope and self-confidence and assist disadvantaged people to compete for whatever work is available. In comparatively prosperous areas, welfare-to-work programmes may counter social isolation and exclusion and challenge the discouraged or disillusioned worker; such programmes might also be better resourced.

Two characteristics of welfare caseloads seemed to have an independent effect on the effectiveness of welfare-to-work programmes in increasing earnings. Programmes targeted on young people or, at least, those in which the average age of participants was under 30 were likely to be much less successful than programmes with older clientele: the difference in the impact on earnings averaged $72.71 per quarter. Similarly, the racial composition of the participant population appeared to be important with the difference in earnings between participants and controls falling by $1.38 for each percentage point increase in the proportion of non-white recipients.[28]

---

[28] Unlike us, Bloom et al (2003) did not find evidence that programme impacts on earnings were affected by the age, race, and ethnicity of programme participants. In addition, they found that programme earnings effects were larger for clients who had been on AFDC for at least a year prior to programme entry and who were secondary school graduates, while we did not. Although the reasons why our findings differ from theirs are not entirely clear and merit further examination, there are at least two possible explanations. First, their findings are based on a subset of the programs included in our study (18 versus 64). It is possible that their findings and ours differ because different samples of programmes were examined.

So, to summarize, work-first programmes appear to have increased wages by more than initiatives that promoted vocational training and the success of welfare-to-work schemes was influenced by local unemployment and poverty rates and by the age and racial composition of benefit caseloads.

Impact on Receipt of AFDC

The second measure of programme performance considered was the impact on claimant caseloads, a factor ostensibly more under the control of programme designers. In fact, as noted in Chapter 5, programmes varied much more in terms of their success in reducing caseloads than in increasing earnings. Again, the impact of programme design was mediated by local economic conditions and by caseload characteristics but, although a larger number of factors appeared to have a bearing on the success or otherwise of a programme, generally each seemed more muted in its effect on caseloads than on earnings. Nonetheless, as in the case of the variance in programme impacts on earnings, over half the variance in caseload reductions could be accounted for by the variables considered.

The pattern of programme characteristics that appear to determine the effectiveness of policy in cutting claimant caseloads differs considerably from those associated with increases in earnings. While sanctioning and participation in job search had statistically significant effects on the receipt of AFDC, the effects were rather small. For example, each percentage point increase in the net sanction rate increased programme impact on receipt of AFDC by 0.1 of a percentage point and even less in the case of job-search. The influence of vocational training was similarly small; but, in contrast with its negative effect on earnings, it was positively associated with larger impacts on caseload reductions.

Further analysis suggests that the effects of these three programme characteristics became more evident over time and were quite strong 21 months or so after people were assigned to the programmes. The implication is that, in the case of job-search and sanctioning, there was a significant delay in re-determining eligibility for benefit after people secured employed or that it took time for wages to increase sufficiently to lift people above the threshold of entitlement. The disparity in the effect of vocational training on wage income and benefit receipt is also explicable to changes over time. The effect on wages emerged early and subsequently subsided suggesting, as already noted, that people lost earnings

---

Second, their study is based on the characteristics of individuals who were randomly assigned (e.g. whether a given individual is white or black), while our study is based on impact estimates drawn from evaluation reports and aggregate measures of participant characteristics (e.g. the percentage of each study sample that was white or black). In principle, the former data should be superior to the latter. However, it is possible that our aggregate measures reflect certain programme- or site-level influences that are missed by variables measured on individuals. For example, if a high proportion of programme participants are black or Hispanic, this suggests that the AFDC population is mainly located in inner cities where relatively few jobs are located. Such an effect should be picked up by aggregate measures of the sort we use, but may not be by data on individuals.

because of participating in training. The later impact on case rolls without a corresponding increase in earnings does not suggest much direct benefit from vocational training. Rather it might reflect the experience of a group of people who were assigned to vocational training but failed to participate, possibly because they were already engaged in undeclared work, and who were eventually dropped from the rolls.

Participation in work experience had a small negative effect on claimant numbers. Each percentage point increase in the net rate of participation in work experience decreased the impact of programmes on AFDC receipt by 0.06 of a percentage point. This probably reflects that fact that most work experience offered on welfare-to-work programmes provides few skills and is unpaid. Hence, work experience does little to help participants move off benefit.

Larger effects were associated with imposition of time limits on the duration of benefit (which not surprisingly led to falls in claimant numbers) and with the offer financial incentives (that had the opposite effect). Higher earnings disregards and more generous minimum income levels, which were typically provided by financial incentives, allowed participants to continue to receive AFDC, when similar programmes without such incentives did not. Thus, inclusion of financial incentives in a welfare-to-work programme reduces its impact on AFDC receipt by 8.6 percentage points but may, of course, have increased both work effort and family incomes. However, it should be noted that provision of financial incentives did not increase impacts on earnings and may actually have reduced them (Greenberg et al., forthcoming). The imposition of time limits on the receipt of AFDC increased impact of programmes on the receipt of AFDC by 3.3 percentage points, even though no more than a handful of people actually reached the time limit in any of the programmes included in the study. Presumably it was the awareness that benefits could be time-limited that encouraged people to leave benefit early or not to reclaim it. Diversion strategies adopted by staff to prevent people from claiming (or needing to claim benefit) have elsewhere been credited with achieving marked reductions in welfare caseloads (Goldsmith and Valvano, 2002; Kaplan, 2002).

Finally, the generosity of AFDC provision locally, assessed by the maximum amount available to a family of three, also served as a constraint on the effectiveness of programmes in reducing caseloads. Programme impacts were reduced by 0.3 of a percentage point with every $100 increase in the benefit level possibly because generous benefits acted as an inducement rather than a deterrent to claiming benefit but also because work effort and earnings could be higher before recipients lost entitlement to AFDC. It should be borne in mind that higher AFDC benefits would also have been available to controls and are not unique to the policy innovation being tested. In a sense, therefore, it is appropriate to consider benefit levels as an aspect of the policy environment comparable to, for example, local unemployment and poverty rates. Equally, though, benefit levels are an integral part of the entire welfare-to-work package and appear, on balance, to impede attempts to reduce caseload size.

The ability of welfare-to-work programmes to reduce caseloads was mediated by caseload composition in a more nuanced way than earnings. Racial composition illustrates this in that the white/non-white distinction evident with respect to the impact of policy on earnings was replaced by subtle differences associated with ethnicity. So for example, with other characteristics held constant, each percentage point increase in the proportion of black participants reduced the impact of a programme by 0.05 of a percentage point. However, the presence of a large proportion of non-white/non-black claimants (a group mainly comprised of Hispanics) had a somewhat larger deflating effect on the success of a programme; the expected fall in caseload was reduced by 0.09 of a percentage point with every additional percentage point increase in the proportion of non-white/non-black claimants.

Likewise, the gender composition of welfare populations had an effect on the ease with which caseloads could be reduced in a way that it did not affect earnings growth. It will be recalled that 93 per cent of all AFDC recipients were lone mothers. Even so, the success of policy innovation in shrinking caseloads was reduced in those administrations with high proportions of female claimants. Each extra percentage point increase in the proportion of female participants reduced programme impact on the receipt of AFDC by 0.15 of a percentage point.

Programmes that included greater numbers of people with recent work experience were also less successful in moving AFDC recipients off the rolls. Recent experience was defined as any employment during the year prior to random assignment and each percentage point increase in the proportion of participants with recent employment reduced the impact on caseload numbers by 0.07 of a percentage point. It is possible that the reason for this is deadweight in that recently employed persons might have been readily able find jobs on their own without aid of a welfare-to-work programme.

Finally, the success of programmes in reducing caseloads was mediated by levels of deprivation locally though not, apparently, by unemployment. Where poverty rates were high, the impact of welfare-to-work programmes was smaller: a percentage point increase in local poverty rates reduced programme impact on AFDC receipt by 0.1 of a percentage point.

Summary: Work-First Scores over Human Capital Approaches

To summarize the findings so far, the meta-evaluation has supported claims of the superiority of a work-first approach, at least with respect to earnings growth, confirming the relative success of so-called 'tough love' embodied in an emphasis on job search strategies and sanctioning. In addition, generous benefits and financial incentives both seemed to limit the effectiveness of programmes in reducing caseloads, while the imposition of time limits on the receipt of benefit appeared to enhance it. However, the analysis also reveals that participant characteristics and site environmental conditions were often equally, and sometimes more, important than programme characteristics in determining the success of welfare-to-work programmes. In general, programmes performed better if their participants included fewer non-whites; women; people aged under 30; and people with recent employment records. In addition, programmes performed better in areas with low unemployment rates, and less generous AFDC payment levels.

The meta-evaluation demonstrates clearly the important and powerful influence of sanctioning on programme impacts. High levels of sanctioning significantly enhanced the effectiveness of programmes in both enhancing participants' earnings and cutting AFDC caseloads. Likewise, a focus on job search seemed to trigger falling caseloads and promote higher earnings while the results of an emphasis on vocational training receipt were at best equivocal and at worse, in relation to earnings, counterproductive. High benefit levels also hindered attempts to cut caseloads while having no measurable effect on earnings.

Yet persuasive though these conclusions may be, they are not the full story. It will be recalled from Chapter 5 that the Riverside programme in California was outstandingly successful and yet was relatively 'soft' on sanctions and located in a state with generous levels of benefit. Likewise, the welfare-to-work programme in Portland, Oregon was almost equally successful and yet incorporated a significant measure of education and training services alongside the focus on job search. Therefore, the twin aims in the next section are first, to consider whether these two outstandingly effective programmes call into question the statistical evidence that supports the contention that 'work first beats training first' and secondly, to determine whether their success owes more to programme design and implementation or to unusual local circumstances.

Why the Riverside and Portland Programmes Excel

Work-first programmes emphasize job search, often with a strong message that even a poorly paid job is better than no job, and that a minimum of education and training will be provided only as a last resort. Human capital programmes use education (particularly adult basic education) and training to upgrade the skills of welfare recipients before they seek work, so that they can obtain stable, well-paid jobs. The Riverside and Portland programmes generally adhered to the work-first model, but differed in several crucial respects both from that model and from each other.

Work-First, with Modifications

Riverside County was one of six counties included as part of the evaluation of California's Greater Avenues for Independence (GAIN), a job search and training programme for AFDC recipients initiated state-wide in 1986. The Riverside programme placed much greater emphasis on work than the other five counties, which to varying degrees adopted a human capital approach, and the strong positive findings for Riverside were widely perceived as a validation of work-first approaches. Unlike most work-first programmes, however, Riverside put much effort into training for those who did not immediately find work and case management and job search services for those who did.

The Portland (Oregon) programme is one of the 11 evaluated programmes included in the National Evaluation of the Welfare-to-Work Strategies (NEWWS) supported by the U.S. Department of Health and Human Services; these programmes vary considerably in their designs.[29] Like most welfare-to-work programmes, Portland emphasized to recipients that their goal is a job. As in human capital programmes, it encouraged clients in need of more skills to enrol in education or training first, and, unlike most welfare-to-work programmes, it encouraged them to wait until they could find a 'good' job.

The impact of the Riverside and Portland programmes participants' earnings and caseload reduction were both much greater than the average for the other sites evaluated – for convenience this average is referred to as the 'typical site' (Table 6.2). In Riverside, those participating in the welfare-to-work experiment (the experimental group) earned on average $300 more than those who did not participate (the control group) in both the third and seventh quarters after they entered the programme; in the typical site, the difference between experimental and control groups was $100 or less. In Portland, the advantage was initially not so great – $189 – in the third quarter, but by the seventh quarter, those participating also earned over $300 more than non-participants. The Portland programme appears to have been more effective than Riverside in moving people off welfare. By the seventh quarter, welfare receipt among Portland participants was down 11.6 percentage points, as compared to the control group; this is six times more than the decline in welfare use at a typical site (less than two percentage points). In Riverside the decline in welfare receipt owing to the programme, 5.3 percentage points, was still considerably more than the decline at the typical site.

If the exceptional performance of Riverside and Portland was not simply due to chance, sampling error, the programmes must have differed systematically from the typical site in some aspects of their design, in the characteristics of participants, or in those of the sites themselves. Compared to a typical site, the welfare-to-work programme in Riverside was characterized by high rates of participation in job search and low use of vocational training and work experience, clearly underlining the substance underpinning the work-first rhetoric (Tables 6.3). However, as noted above though not widely appreciated, sanction rates were relatively low and the use of basic education services comparatively high.

In terms of site characteristics, participants in Riverside tended to be older than the norm and more likely to be employed at the time they were assigned to experimental status; a larger proportion was white (51 per cent versus 37 per cent for the typical site) and a somewhat smaller proportion female. Finally, the poverty rate in Riverside was substantially lower than that in the typical site

---

[29] Congress mandated the large-scale evaluation of 11 welfare-to-work programmes in 7 sites. The National Evaluation of the Welfare-to-Work Strategies (NEWWS) included a two-wave survey of all grantees, implementation studies through site visits, and studies of participant outcomes. Findings are posted on the Web site of the Assistant Secretary for Planning and Evaluation in the Department of Health and Human Services, http://aspe.os.dhhs.gov/hsp/NEWWS/.

Table 6.2   Programme effects on earnings and AFDC receipt for a 'typical site', Riverside and Portland

	'Typical Site'			Effects		Differences from 'Typical Site'	
	Number	Effects	Standard Deviation	Riverside	Portland	Riverside	Portland
Earnings ($)							
3rd Quarter after RA	53	79.32	80.04	300.05	189.04	220.73	109.72
7th Quarter after RA	52	101.15	103.33	340.32	337.90	239.17	236.75
AFDC Receipt (%)							
3rd Quarter after RA	41	1.66	3.57	3.90	6.80	2.24	5.14
7th Quarter after RA	49	1.95	4.73	5.30	11.60	3.35	9.65

Note: RA = Random Assignment

Table 6.3 Values of the explanatory variables used in the quarter 3 earnings regressions for a 'typical site' and for Riverside and Portland

	'Typical Site'		Observed values		Differences from 'Typical Site'	
	Mean	Standard Deviation	Riverside	Portland	Riverside	Portland
NET PROGRAMME EFFECT ON % RECEIVING						
Sanctions	8.69	9.74	6.00	14.00	-2.69	5.31
Job Search	21.18	11.91	36.60	32.20	15.42	11.02
Basic Education	6.13	10.33	18.20	5.30	12.07	-0.83
Vocational Training	2.77	4.55	-1.80	7.30	-4.57	4.53
Work Experience	3.09	5.36	-0.60	7.10	-3.69	4.01
PROGRAMME INCLUDES						
Financial Incentives	0.27	0.42	0.00	0.00	-0.27	-0.27
Time Limits	0.13	0.32	0.00	0.00	-0.13	-0.13
PART CHARACTERISTICS						
% White	37.27	21.92	51.20	69.60	13.97	32.33
% Female	90.99	5.31	88.00	93.20	-2.99	2.21
% Employed in year before RA						
Average age<30	0.39	0.47	0.00	0.00	-0.39	-0.39
% Under age 25	27.99	23.43	10.20	22.70	-17.79	-5.29

Table 6.3 continued

	'Typical Site'		Observed values			Differences from 'Typical Site'	
	Mean	Standard Deviation	Riverside	Portland		Riverside	Portland
PART CHARACTERISTICS							
% High School Degree	51.06	8.55	51.40	55.30		0.34	4.24
Average Number of Children	1.92	0.28	1.80	2.00		-0.12	0.08
SITE CHARACTERISTICS							
Unemployment rate	6.65	2.56	6.70	4.30		0.05	-2.35
Poverty rate	15.53	4.76	10.80	14.30		-4.73	-1.23
Poverty rate squared	241.18	160.72	116.64	204.49		-124.54	-36.69
Max AFDC Payments	541.07	201.51	782.00	538.00		240.93	-3.07
% Manufacturing Employment	12.53	4.75	8.60	10.60		-3.93	-1.93
Medium HH income	39398.74	6888.44	38705.00	37865.00		-693.74	-1533.74
Number of years since 1982	9.84	3.83	11.00	11.00		1.16	1.16

Note: RA = Random Assignment. Net programme effects on sanctions and receipt of services are estimated by deducting the relevant control group values from the relevant programme group values. Site and participant characteristics are means. The 'average age<30' is a dummy variable that equals one if the average age of the programme group was under 30 and zero if the average age above 30 for individual sites; it will assume a value between zero and one if averaged across sites.

(11 compared to 16 per cent in the third quarter after random assignment), while the unemployment rate (7 percent) in Riverside was virtually identical to that in the typical site in the third quarter.

The Portland programme, like Riverside's, placed much more emphasis on job search than the typical site, but incorporated a larger measure of education and training services. Where Riverside focused on basic education, Portland's programme emphasized vocational training and work experience, and its sanction rates were high – almost twice those in the typical site. Neither Riverside nor Portland provided any financial incentives; nor did the programmes incorporate time limits. The proportion of participants in Portland who were white was much larger (nearly 70 percent) that at a typical site. The poverty rate stood at 14.3 per cent in the seventh quarter, and unemployment in the area was much lower (4.3 percent).

Explaining Success

The differences between Portland and Riverside and the typical site, which are summarized in Table 6.3, may be used together with explanatory regression analyses discussed in the first part of this chapter to mathematically explain what factors contributed to unusual success of the Portland and Riverside programmes.[30] The results of such an exercise are given Tables 6.4 and 6.5 for the impact on earnings and welfare caseloads respectively. Both tables record the absolute and percentage contribution of each factor to the observed difference between the outcomes of Portland and Riverside and those of the typical site. Thus, the top left-hand cell in Table 6.4 indicates that the low level of sanctioning in Riverside reduced the effectiveness of the programme in boosting wages in the third quarter after random assignment by the equivalent of $12 in the third calendar quarter after random assignment or by about five per cent. Clearly this shortfall was made up by other factors notably job-search which had the effect of increasing wages relative to the typical site by $48 in the third quarter after random assignment.

Several features of programme design seem to have made important contributions to Riverside and Portland's exceptionally large impacts on earnings. These include the strong emphasis in both sites on job search, the heavy

---

[30] Multiplying each of the differences between Riverside and Portland and a 'typical site' (last two columns of Table 6.3) by the corresponding regression coefficient (first or second column of Annex 6A), indicates by how much each factor contributed to the exceptionally large earnings impacts found in Riverside and Portland in the 3rd quarter. A similar procedure is used to examine the factors that account for Riverside and Portland's exceptional performance in increasing earnings in the 7th quarter and in reducing the receipt of AFDC in the 3rd and 7th quarters. The findings from this exercise, which are based on estimates from the Model 1 regressions in Annexes 6A and 6B, are shown in Tables 6.4 and 6.5 for earnings and the receipt of AFDC, respectively. These tables report both the absolute and the percentage contributions of each factor to the total observed differences between the impacts of Riverside and Portland on earnings and the receipt of AFDC and those of a 'typical site,' which are shown in the last two columns of Table 6.2.

Table 6.4 Estimates* of the influence of programme and contextual characteristics on the difference in programme effects on earnings between Riverside/Portland and a 'typical site'

| | QUARTER 3 | | | | QUARTER 7 | | | |
| | Riverside | | Portland | | Riverside | | Portland | |
	Absolute	%	Absolute	%	Absolute	%	Absolute	%
EFFECT ON % RECEIVING								
Sanctions	-12.00	-5.43	23.68	21.58	-16.43	-6.86	29.53	12.48
Job Search	48.08	21.78	34.36	31.32	30.73	12.82	21.97	9.28
Basic education	-19.70	-8.92	1.36	1.24	-5.29	-2.21	0.90	0.38
Vocational Training	33.17	15.03	-32.88	-29.97	21.18	8.84	-19.06	-8.05
Work experience	7.67	3.47	-8.33	-7.60	-4.64	-1.94	4.91	2.07
PROGRAMME INCLUDES								
Financial Incentives	12.29	5.57	12.29	11.20	17.37	7.25	17.37	7.34
PARTICIPANT CHARACTERISTICS								
% White	22.72	10.29	52.73	48.06	9.24	3.85	27.93	11.80
Average age<30	18.68	8.46	18.68	17.02	31.27	13.05	31.27	13.21
SITE CHARACTERISTICS								
Unemployment rate	0.16	0.07	-7.53	-6.86	-9.53	-3.98	24.66	10.42
Poverty rate	175.94	79.71	45.75	41.70	87.77	36.62	42.04	17.75
Poverty rate squared	-147.83	-66.97	-43.55	-39.69	-67.48	-28.15	-34.23	-14.46

* Derived from Model 1 in Annex 6.1

Table 6.5 Estimates* of the influence of programme and contextual characteristics on the difference in programme effects on AFDC receipt between Riverside/Portland and a 'typical site'

| | QUARTER 3 | | | | QUARTER 7 | | | |
| | Riverside | | Portland | | Riverside | | Portland | |
	Absolute	%	Absolute	%	Absolute	%	Absolute	%
EFFECT ON % RECEIVING								
Sanctions	-0.05	-2.43	0.13	2.49	-0.55	-16.58	0.82	8.50
Job Search	0.97	43.12	0.68	13.29	1.29	38.58	0.93	9.60
Basic education	0.11	4.90	-0.02	-0.49	-0.48	-14.33	0.11	1.13
Vocational Training	-0.33	-14.82	0.31	6.10	-1.78	-53.36	1.43	14.86
Work experience	0.25	11.15	-0.20	-3.82	0.59	17.80	-0.48	-4.99
PROGRAMME INCLUDES								
Financial incentives	2.09	93.23	2.09	40.63	2.25	67.41	2.26	23.40
Time limits	-0.63	-28.18	-0.63	-12.28	-0.18	-5.39	-0.18	-1.87
PARTICIPANT CHARACTERISTICS								
% White	0.81	36.25	2.01	39.11	0.78	23.40	2.21	22.94
% Female	0.84	37.63	-0.05	-1.00	0.80	24.08	-0.28	-2.90
% Employed in year prior to R.A.	-0.94	-42.09	0.14	2.70	-1.18	-35.37	0.18	1.91
% Under age 25	-1.47	-65.59	-0.43	-8.50	-0.22	-6.84	-0.07	-0.82

* Derived from Model 1 in Annex 6.2

Table 6.6   Summary statistics for the influence of programme and contextual characteristics on the difference in programme effects between Riverside/Portland and a 'typical site'*

	QUARTER 3				QUARTER 7			
	Riverside		Portland		Riverside		Portland	
	Absolute	%	Absolute	%	Absolute	%	Absolute	%
EARNINGS								
1) Total observed difference	220.73	100.00	109.72	100.00	239.17	100.00	236.75	100.00
2) Total 'explained' difference	139.18	63.05	96.55	88.00	94.17	39.29	147.28	62.21
3) Due to programme design	69.52	31.49	30.47	27.77	42.91	17.90	55.63	23.50
4) Due to other factors	69.66	31.56	66.08	60.23	51.26	21.39	91.65	38.71
5) Unexplained difference	81.55	36.95	13.17	12.00	145.00	60.71	89.47	37.79
AFDC RECEIPT								
1) Total observed difference	2.24	100.00	5.14	100.00	3.35	100.00	9.65	100.00
2) Total 'explained' difference	1.64	73.17	4.02	78.21	1.32	39.39	6.93	71.76
3) Due to programme design	2.40	106.97	2.36	45.90	1.14	34.12	4.89	50.62
4) Due to other factors	-0.76	-33.80	1.66	32.31	0.18	5.27	2.04	21.14
5) Unexplained difference	0.60	26.83	1.12	21.79	2.03	60.61	2.72	28.24

* Derived from Model 1 in Annexes 6.1 and 6.2

application of sanctions in Portland, and the limited use made of vocational training in Riverside (which, if used, would generally have lessened the increase in wages experienced by participants). This, of course, is exactly what did happen in Portland where exceptional reliance on vocational training reduced gains in wages by 30 per cent in the third quarter and by 19 per cent in the seventh quarter after entry into the programme. The fact that the caseloads in both sites were somewhat older than was typical and mostly white also contributed to the large increases achieved in wages; but site characteristics, such as the local unemployment and poverty rates, do not seem to have been important.

The strong emphasis on participation in job search in both Portland and (especially) the Riverside programmes also contributed to their above average success in reducing AFDC caseloads, while the decision in each case not to instigate financial incentives such as increased earnings disregards proved to be a judicious one. Success was again boosted by the fact that caseloads in each case were mostly white and, in Riverside, contained a relatively high proportion of male-headed families. On the other hand, in Riverside these advantages were partially offset by the comparatively high proportion of clients who had worked during the year prior to random assignment. Differences in site socio-environmental characteristics (e.g., unemployment rates, medium household income, the poverty rate, and percentage employed in manufacturing) between Riverside (or Portland) and a 'typical site' again proved to be unimportant.

While this analysis suggests that the exceptional success of the Riverside and Portland programmes in increasing earnings and reducing the receipt of AFDC is due to a mix of factors, it is important to establish the extent to which the apparent effectiveness was attributable to programme design as opposed to the characteristics of participants and local environment. The relative contribution of programme design is apparent from Table 6.6, which apportions the difference in impact between Riverside and Portland and a typical site to programme design and other factors.[31] The table is divided into two panels: the top one relating to earnings the bottom to AFDC receipt derived from the Model 1 regressions reported in Annex 6.1 and 6.2 respectively. Row 2 in each panel indicates the extent to which the success of the Riverside and Portland models, compared with

---

[31] Table 6.6 is divided into two panels: the top one relating to earnings the bottom to AFDC receipt derived from the Model 1 regressions reported in Annex 6A and 6B respectively. Row 1 in each panel shows the total observed differences between program impacts in Riverside and Portland and those in a 'typical site'. These values also appear in Table 2, Row 2, which is computed by summing each column in Tables 6.4 and 6.5, indicates the extent to which the associated regressions reported in Annex 6A and 6B successfully 'explain' these differences. Row 3, which is computed for the first and third panels by summing the first six rows in Table 6.4 and the first seven rows in Table 6.5, indicates the part of each 'explained' difference attributable to program design. Similarly, row 4, which is computed by summing remaining rows in Tables 6.4 and 6.5, indicates the part due to participant and site characteristics. Finally, row 5 (row 1 minus row 2) shows the part of observed difference that cannot be explained by the regressions. A similarly constructed table is presented at Annex 6.3 based on the Model 2 regressions reported in Annexes 6.1 and 6.2.

the typical site, can be explained statistically (by reference to the regression models reported in Annex 6.1 and 6.2). With the exception of the caseload reduction in Riverside in the 7th quarter, between two-thirds to three-quarters of the observed difference is explicable.

The key finding – compare rows 3 and 4 in the top panel in Table 6.6 – is that client and site characteristics were at least as important as programme design in accounting for Riverside and Portland's extraordinary success in increasing the earnings of programme participants. In contrast, it appears that the unusual effectiveness of Riverside and Portland programmes in reducing AFDC rolls was primarily the result of programme design features. Indeed, in Riverside, client and site characteristics actually tended to reduce programme impact on AFDC receipt when measured in the 3rd quarter following random assignment. Thus, it appears that the design of the programmes in Riverside and Portland contributed considerably more to their relatively large impacts on AFDC receipt than to their exceptionally sizable impacts on earnings. This could suggest, perhaps not surprisingly, that those responsible for administering AFDC can exercise more control over whether recipients continue to receive benefits than over the earnings that recipients receive.

Therefore to return to the two questions posed at the end of the previous section, the reason why Riverside and Portland programmes were successful reflected both programme design and local conditions. Moreover, in terms of earnings growth, local factors (especially the characteristics of the client population) were as important as design which reinforces the oft forgotten truism that attempts to replicate one policy model in a different environment is unlikely to yield identical results. Indeed, given that local factors have been shown to matter, the evidence points to the need for multiple solutions, rather than a one fits all approach to welfare-to-work. Moreover, the Portland and Riverside models were noticeably different from the classic 'work-first' approach and from each other. Both emphasized job search but supported this with basic education for those who needed it in Riverside and vocational training in Portland. Portland coupled a priority on securing 'good jobs' with a heavy use of sanctions while Riverside blended harsh rhetoric with softer implementation. The modelling treated these components independently although it may be their interaction that is truly important.

It is important not to overstate the power of the models, efficient though they were in statistical terms. Between a quarter and a third of the apparent success of Portland and Riverside – occasionally more – is left unexplained. This 'unexplained error' is probably due in part to differences in programme design and implementation that are inherently difficult to measure and were hence omitted: factors such as leadership, staff attitudes and the quality of communication between staff and participants. Information on client and site characteristics was limited and that available was not always amenable to precise measurement. Some error will also be attributable to sampling because estimates of programme impacts rely on samples from the programmes' target populations and, hence, are not statistically precise. Even so, one can have confidence that policy did make a difference in programme success in increasing earnings and reducing caseload.

The question to be addressed in the final section is whether these effects were long term.

How Long the Benefits Last

Part of the debate between the protagonists of work first and training first approaches has focussed on the most appropriate time at which to measure policy impacts. It is sometimes argued, for example, that work first strategies, by encouraging people rapidly into work, increase wages income in the short term but do not provide secure employment and good prospects. If, because of training, people succeed in finding better jobs they may enjoy higher wages in the longer term. The evidence from the meta-analysis is that there is some truth in this thesis but not enough, at least with respect to welfare recipients in the United States, to refute the notion that work first is a viable or, indeed, preferable option.

The regression analyses employed in the first part of this chapter to explore the factors that contributed to the success of welfare-to-work programmes all included two terms to take into account how long after the random assignment of the programme and control groups programme impacts were measured (see, for example, Table 6.1). The terms were highly statistically significant and point to a distinctive profile in the effectiveness of an intervention that can be represented as an inverted U. The earnings of programme participants first tend to increase relative to randomly assigned controls in the quarters following random assignment, apparently mainly due to participants finding jobs more quickly. Thereafter, the competitive advantage of programme participants declines and eventually disappears as welfare beneficiaries assigned to the control group make their own way into employment, perhaps assisted by the basic services that they are allowed to access. However, this process takes some time to play out. The increase for a typical welfare-to-work programme continues for two to three years, while the decline takes at least another three years, and perhaps longer. Hence, programme effects on earnings appear to persist for five to six years. This is considerably longer than the length of the follow up period for most programme evaluations, and, thus, should be viewed with some caution. Nevertheless, the finding appears robust to a number of alternative regression specifications (Greenberg et al., 2004). An important implication of this finding is that decisions about welfare-to-work programmes should take account of the possibility that their effects on earnings may last for some time. Ignoring this possibility may result in seriously undervaluing the policy interventions in question.

The signature inverted U shape is evident in Figure 6.1, which summarizes the outcome of a quite sophisticated statistical analysis. It similarly demonstrates the persistence of programme effects – in this case on earnings – that first increase in size and then decline over time. However, it additionally allows the profiles of work-first and training first approaches to be considered.

Figure 6.1   **Regression of welfare-to-work programme effects on earnings (quarters 1–23 after random assignment)**

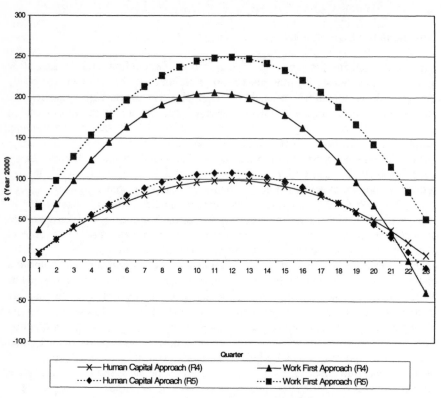

Specifically, Figure 6.1 plots four curves based on predictions of the impact of programme interventions on earnings based on two regression analyses. In the first (coded R4), welfare-to-work programmes were categorized into 'work-first' and 'human capital' approaches on the basis of whether or not the net effect of a programme was to increase job search activities by more or less than the sample mean of 22.2 percentage points. Of course, as the Riverside and Portland examples aptly demonstrated, programmes both differ along a continuum and make use of various combinations of interventions. Thus, this distinction is somewhat arbitrary. Hence, in the second regression, a tighter definition (R5) was imposed such that to count as 'work-first' a programme both had to increase job search activity by more than the mean effect *and* not raise vocational training by as much as average. Less than one-third of programmes met this more stringent definition of 'work first' compared with about half using the less stringent R4 one.

Taking the first definition first, the earnings effects of the fifty or so per cent of programmes emphasising the human capital approach are predicted initially to be quite small: $25 in the second quarter, for example. However, this effect grows until almost the end of the 11th quarter after random assignment, reaching a peak of $99. The earnings effect then falls, reaching zero in the 24th quarter. As expected, the initial earnings effects predicted for programmes relying on a work first approach are considerably larger ($69 in the second quarter). The impact subsequently increases until the beginning of the 11th quarter, reaching a peak of $206, and then declines until zero is reached in the 22nd quarter. Hence, Regression 4 implies that the work first approach initially produces much larger effects on earnings than the human capital approach, but that these effects fall faster once the maximum is reached. By the 21st quarter, the earnings effects of programmes that adopt a human capital approach are predicted to exceed that of programmes characterized as being 'work first' and, hence, to last for slightly longer. However, the additional earnings attributable to either kind of programme after 21 quarters is negligible – just $22 per quarter.

Similar differential profiles are evident from Figure 6.1 based on the stricter formulation of 'work-first'; work-first programmes continue to out-perform ones based on a human capital approach. According to the predictions by the second quarter after random assignment a typical work first programme has a much larger effect on earnings than a typical human capital programme – $98 versus $25 – and continues to do so until near the end of the 11th quarter when both approaches achieve their maximum effect – $250 and $108, respectively. However, after the 11th quarter, the earnings effect falls more quickly under the work first approach, reaching zero in the 24th quarter. Nonetheless, while the human capital approach gains ground relative to the work first approach, it never quite catches up and, in any case, by this time, six years after random assignment, the effect of both types of programme has shrunk to near zero. As a result, the additional earnings attributable to the typical work first programme over 24 quarters ($4,134) far outweigh those achieved by programmes emphasising human capital development ($1,567).

It should be stressed that this analysis is not based on direct observation but on predictions derived from special regression analyses derived from statistical models similar to those presented above. Moreover, the comparisons between work-first and training-first programmes are not based on random assignment.[32] Thus, it is theoretically possible that participants in the two types of programmes differ and that these differences in participant characteristics account for the apparent superiority of the work-first approach. However, there is no evidence that participants in the two types of programmes systematically differ. Indeed, both types of programmes were mandatory and both tended to exclude somewhat similar types of individuals – for example, single mothers with very young children. Moreover, the regression framework controlled for important observable differences in participant characteristics among the evaluated programmes in the sample. One can be fairly certain therefore that, though the individual earnings attributed to welfare-to-work programmes in the United States may be modest, the

---

[32] However, comparisons in three sites that *were* based on random assignment also indicated that programmes that stress human capital investment have smaller impacts than programmes that use a work-first approach (see Hamilton, et al., 1997).

advantage accrued persists over many years.   Moreover, the evidence suggests
consistently that a leaning to work-first type strategies, rather than investing in
human capital, has the larger payoff.

Conclusion

US welfare-to-work programmes have been taken as models of successful social
intervention and many policy analysts and policy makers in Britain (as well as the
US) now hold the view that work-first approaches are the most effective strategies
for reducing welfare dependency.

The meta-evaluation of exclusively US evidence reported in this chapter
confirms the relative success of the 'tough love' approach embodied in an
emphasis on job search strategies and sanctioning and, thus, supports claims of the
superiority of a work-first approach.   However, it also reveals that participant
characteristics and local socio-economic conditions are often equally, and
sometimes even more, important than programme characteristics in determining
the success of welfare-to-work programmes.   In general, programmes proved to be
more effective when caseloads included comparative few women; non-whites;
people aged under 30; and people with recent employment records.   Programmes
also performed better when located in areas with low unemployment and less
poverty.

Sanctions have been lauded as a keystone to the success of US welfare-to-
work programmes and have been critical to policy thinking and development in the
US and the UK (Lødemel and Trickey, 2001).   The meta-evaluation demonstrates
clearly the important and powerful influence of sanctioning on programme
effectiveness.   Programme impacts on both participants' earnings and AFDC
receipt were significantly enhanced by welfare-to-work regimes that utilized a high
level of sanctioning.   However, the Riverside programme in California succeeded
despite, in fact, being relatively 'soft' on sanctions.   Its below-average net
sanctioning rate reduced its impact, but this negative effect was small and it did not
prevent Riverside from achieving amongst the highest earnings increases and
largest reduction in AFDC receipt of all the welfare-to-work programmes that have
been subject to rigorous evaluation.

Generous welfare payments have been suspected of increasing welfare
dependency, but the meta-evaluation provided only limited evidence to support this
claim.   Although above average AFDC payments seemed to reduce programme
impact on the receipt of AFDC, this effect was small, and high levels of payments
did not affect programme earnings impacts.   Again, the Riverside programme
serves as a model of successful programme implementation despite the high
average AFDC payments in California.

The offer of financial incentives mainly increased earnings disregards.   As
a result, financial incentives seem to delay the process of moving off AFDC, as
would be expected, but perhaps unexpectedly also failed to have a positive
influence on programme impacts on earnings.   However, financial incentives can
conceivably increase income (i.e., earnings plus AFDC) and thus might reduce

poverty. Different impact indicators than the ones used in this study would be required to assess the wider effects of incentives.

In contrast to incentives, the imposition of time limits on the receipt of AFDC appears to have accelerated the process of leaving AFDC rolls. Given that few participants actually reached the time limits during the evaluations of the programmes that had them, the mechanism that leads to this outcome is not well understood and warrants further study.

In general, the findings from this meta-evaluation suggest that welfare-to-work programmes work best when they employ work-first approaches that focus on job search activities, and resort to sanctioning and impose time limits. But they also point to important qualifications.

First, the effectiveness of programmes is not just a matter of programme design and implementation but is also influenced by the characteristics of programme participants and socio-economic conditions. The importance of these factors and their variability across programmes and programme sites call for flexible approaches to programme development. Supporting measures may be put into place to help programmes overcome obstacles posed by the racial, gender, or age composition of their participants. This may involve additional government agencies, or might be achieved through programme providers.

Secondly, socio-economic variations call for different area-based approaches. In relatively advantaged areas, programmes may want to target resources on particularly disadvantaged individuals or neighbourhoods. Conversely, in areas with few advantageous socio-economic characteristics or high unemployment, saturation may be preferable to targeting to ensure that programme activities reach deeply into these communities.

Thirdly, the analysis indicates that it is a combination of factors that determine the success or failure of welfare-to-work programmes. As noted above, the programme tested in Riverside California enjoyed exceptional success but succeeded both because of *and* despite of its mix of services and sanctions and the social and economic circumstances in which it operated. Sanctions, to give but one example, may thus be a 'supportive' but not a 'necessary' component of welfare-to-work programmes. In Portland, heavy sanctioning was used alongside a programme that encouraged participants to seek better jobs even if, on occasion, this meant a longer period of searching.

Finally, the US experience is that, although the financial benefits that accrue to individuals through participation in welfare-to-work schemes are, on average, modest, they nevertheless persist over many years. Wage gains continue to increase for almost three years, on average, before the impact of programmes begins to decline and finally to peter out after five or six years. By then, participants in work-first programmes may well have gained more than $4,000 in additional wages although some of this financial benefit will have been dissipated by loss of entitlement to benefits.

References

Ashworth, K., Cebulla, A., Greenberg, D. and Walker, R. (2004), 'Meta-evaluation: Discovering What Works Best in Welfare Provision', *Evaluation,* Vol. 10.2, pp. 193-216.

Bloom, H.S., Hill, C.J. and Riccio, J. (2003), 'Linking programme implementation and effectiveness: Lessons from a pooled sample of welfare-to-work experiments', *Journal of Policy Analysis and Management,* Vol. 22.4, pp. 551-575.

Goldsmith, D. and Valvano, V. (2002), *TANF Diversion: An effective strategy for helping families remain off assistance?* Paper presented at the NAWRS 42nd Annual Workshop Albuquerque, New Mexico, August 27.

Greenberg, D., Michalopoulos, C. and Robins, P.K. (2003), 'A meta-analysis of government-sponsored training programmes', *Industrial and Labor Relations Review,* Vol. 57.1, pp. 31-53.

Greenberg, D., Ashworth, K., Cebulla, A. and Walker, R. (2004a), *When welfare-to-work programmes seem to work well: Explaining why Riverside and Portland shine so brightly,* mimeo, Centre for Research in Social Policy, Loughborough.

Greenberg, D., Ashworth, K., Cebulla, A. and Walker, R. (2004b), 'Do welfare-to-work programmes work for long?', *Fiscal Studies,* Vol 25.1, pp. 27-53.

Hamilton, G., Brock, T., Farrell, M., Friedlander, D. and Harkett, K. (1997), *Evaluating Two Welfare-to-Work Programme Approaches: Two-year findings on the labor force attachment and human capital development programmes in three sites,* US Department of Health and Human Services and US Department of Education, Washington, D.C.

Kaplan, J. (2002), 'Applicant Diversion – Recent Developments', *WIN (Welfare Information Network) Resources for Welfare Decisions,* Vol. 6.11, July; www.financeprojectinfo.org/Publications/applicantdiversionRN.htm, visited 15th June 2004.

Lødemel, I. and Trickey, H. (2001), *'An Offer You Can't Refuse': Workfare in an international perspective,* Policy Press, Bristol.

Mead, L.M. (2004), *Government Matters: Welfare Reform in Wisconsin,* Princeton University Press, Princeton.

Walker, R. (1991), *Thinking about Workfare: Learning from US experience,* HMSO, London.

Walker, R., Greenberg, D., Ashworth, K. and Cebulla, A. (2003), 'Successful welfare-to-work programmes: Were Riverside and Portland really that good?', *Focus, Journal of the Institute for Research on Poverty, University of Madison-Wisconsin,* Vol. 22.3, pp. 1-8.

Annex 6.1   Weighted regression estimates for programme effects on earnings (3rd and 7th quarters after random assignment)

	MODEL 1		MODEL 2	
	Quarter 3	Quarter 7	Quarter 3	Quarter 7
Constant	227.18 *	333.01 *	972.56 **	951.05 *
	(122.62)	(153.61)	(429.77)	(505.60)
EFFECT ON % RECEIVING				
Sanctions	4.46 ***	5.75 ***	3.24 **	3.44
	(1.03)	(1.34)	(1.23)	(2.20)
Job Search	3.12 ***	1.99 *	3.36 ***	2.71 **
	(0.95)	(0.97)	(1.14)	(1.27)
Basic Education	-1.63	-0.48	-2.50 *	-1.88
	(1.11)	(1.11)	(1.35)	(1.43)
Vocational Training	-7.26 ***	-4.42	-4.55	.48
	(2.50)	(2.54)	(3.09)	(3.27)
Work Experience	-2.08	1.24	0.81	5.30
	(2.11)	(2.39)	(2.45)	(3.14)
PROGRAMME INCLUDES				
Financial Incentives	-45.53	-66.79 *	-41.16	-168.07 ***
	(28.54)	(33.36)	(36.36)	(44.82)
Time Limit			-4.08	111.34 **
			(43.13)	(51.68)
PARTICIPANT CHARACTERISTICS				
% White	1.63 ***	1.02	0.84	0.64
	(0.56)	(0.58)	(0.74)	(0.79)
% Female			-1.68	-0.20
			(1.89)	(2.17)
% Employed in Year Prior to R.A.			0.19	-2.74 *
			(0.98)	(1.37)

Annex 6.1 continued

	MODEL 1		MODEL 2	
	Quarter 3	Quarter 7	Quarter 3	Quarter 7
Average age < 30 = 1	-47.89 **	-76.27 ***	-20.64	36.08
	(22.31)	(23.42)	(33.76)	(42.34)
% High School Degree			-5.01 **	1.03
			(2.32)	(2.37)
Average Number of Children			-7.86	-104.98
			(76.50)	(85.78)
SITE CHARACTERISTICS				
Unemployment Rate	3.20	-10.36 *	1.27	-11.70 **
	(4.40)	(4.91)	(4.72)	(5.23)
Poverty Rate	-37.20 **	-28.59	-54.18 ***	-67.61 ***
	(15.21)	(17.82)	(19.12)	(24.19)
Poverty Rate squared	1.19 ***	0.82	1.52 ***	1.88 ***
	(0.45)	(0.52)	(0.53)	(0.67)
Maximum AFDC Payment			0.11	0.22 *
			(0.09)	(0.11)
% Manufacturing Employment			-2.87	-6.31
			(2.79)	(3.51)
Median Household Income (In $1000s)			-0.01 **	-0.01
			(0.00)	(0.00)
Number of Years Since 1982			5.76	12.25 **
			(4.05)	(5.35)
$\overline{R}^2$	.337	.413	.567	.508
Number of Observations	53	52	53	52

*** Significant at the 1 per cent level, ** Significant at the 5 per cent level, * Significant at the 10 per cent level.

Annex 6.2 Weighted regression estimates for programme effects on AFDC receipt (3rd and 7th quarters after random assignment)

	MODEL 1		MODEL 2	
	Quarter 3	Quarter 7	Quarter 3	Quarter 7
Constant	16.716	21.660 **	26.350	22.280
	(11.131)	(10.220)	(25.560)	(30.120)
EFFECT ON % RECEIVING				
Sanctions	0.023	0.172 ***	-0.065	0.125
	(0.052)	(0.062)	(0.060)	(0.086)
Job Search	0.064	0.083 *	0.039	0.168 **
	(0.043)	(0.049)	(0.058)	(0.081)
Basic Education	0.010	-0.046	0.048	-0.018
	(0.047)	(0.059)	(0.059)	(0.081)
Vocational Training	0.071	0.354 **	-0.116	0.349
	(0.135)	(0.162)	(0.157)	(0.217)
Work Experience	-0.058	-0.140	0.217	-0.063
	(0.100)	(0.120)	(0.150)	(0.199)
PROGRAMME INCLUDES				
Financial Incentives	-7.735 ***	-7.787 ***	-10.555 ***	-7.527 ***
	(1.478)	(1.517)	(1.932)	(2.512)
Time Limit	5.739 ***	2.581	6.071 ***	2.751
	(1.861)	(2.447)	(1.996)	(2.824)
PARTICIPANT CHARACTERISTICS				
% White	0.065 **	0.078 ***	0.046	0.088 *
	(0.028)	(0.029)	(0.035)	(0.047)
% Female	-0.172	-0.209 *	-0.305 **	-0.271 **
	(0.114)	(0.106)	(0.124)	(0.129)
% Employed in Year Prior to R.A.	-0.105 **	-0.133 ***	-0.100 *	-0.135 **
	(0.045)	(0.050)	(0.051)	(0.065)

Annex 6.2 continued

	MODEL 1		MODEL 2	
	Quarter 3	Quarter 7	Quarter 3	Quarter 7
PART CHARACTERISTICS				
% Under Age 25	0.082 **	0.012	0.244 ***	-0.006
	(0.031)	(0.034)	(0.080)	(0.100)
% High School Degree			-0.075	-0.064
			(0.096)	(0.121)
Average Number of Children			11.821	-2.623
			(5.99)	(7.964)
SITE CHARACTERISTICS				
Unemployment Rate			-0.450 *	-0.049
			(0.241)	(0.331)
Poverty Rate			-0.749	1.288
			(0.883)	(1.388)
Poverty Rate squared			0.016	-0.038
			(0.024)	(0.038)
Max AFDC Payment (In $100s)			0.237	-0.564
			(0.456)	(0.643)
% Manufacturing Employment			-0.217 *	0.119
			(0.121)	(0.189)
Median Household Income ($1000s)			-0.188	0.002
			(0.132)	(0.167)
Number of Years Since 1982			0.132	0.366
			(0.202)	(0.248)
$\overline{R}^2$	.360	.392	.467	.460
Number of Observations	41	49	41	49

*** Significant at the 1 per cent level, ** Significant at the 5 per cent level, * Significant at the 10 per cent level.

Annex 6.3   Summary statistics for the influence of programme and contextual characteristics on the difference in programme effects between Riverside/Portland and a 'typical site'

| | QUARTER 3 | | | | QUARTER 7 | | | |
| | Riverside | | Portland | | Riverside | | Portland | |
	Absolute	%	Absolute	%	Absolute	%	Absolute	%
EARNINGS								
1) Total observed difference	220.73	100.00	109.72	100.00	239.17	100.00	236.75	100.00
2) Total 'explained' difference	182.15	82.52	87.85	80.07	191.51	79.90	175.97	74.33
3) Due to programme design	42.30	19.16	50.51	46.04	68.74	28.68	105.23	44.45
4) Due to other factors	139.85	63.36	37.34	34.03	122.77	51.22	70.74	29.88
5) Unexplained difference	38.58	17.48	21.87	19.93	47.66	20.10	60.78	25.67
AFDC RECEIPT: MODEL 2								
1) Total observed difference	2.24	100.00	5.14	100.00	3.35	100.00	9.65	100.00
2) Total 'explained' difference	2.63	117.36	6.37	123.89	1.41	42.08	7.78	80.64
3) Due to programme design	3.04	135.54	2.33	45.40	2.51	75.08	5.69	59.00
4) Due to other factors	-0.41	-18.18	4.04	78.49	-1.11	-33.00	2.09	21.64
5) Unexplained difference	-0.39	-17.36	-1.23	-23.89	1.94	57.92	1.87	19.36

Note: Derived from Model 2 in Annexes 6.1 and 6.2

Chapter 7

Looking over the Fence: Findings from UK and US Programme Reviews

Andreas Cebulla

Introduction

This chapter reviews some of the evaluation evidence pertaining to labour market programmes that was not covered in the meta-analysis. Evidence from our meta-analysis reported in earlier chapters has suggested that programmes, which aim to place participants into jobs quickly, are more effective than programmes, which place greater emphasis on training and the development of human resources. Here, the evolution of training and job placement programmes in place in the UK prior to the New Deal is charted and the key lessons from their evaluations are discussed. Systematic review evidence from US job training programmes is also presented.

Although past evaluations of UK training and placement programmes and more recent evaluations of the New Deal are not immediately comparable because of differences in the timing and location of these programmes and pilot programmes as well as because of variations in their target populations, most studies convey similar conclusions and policy message. Yet, comparisons with recent US evaluations and, in particular, meta-evaluations also suggest a continued need for the greater disaggregating of impact measurements, which would improve our understanding of the key features that determine effective welfare-to-work policy.

The chapter also takes a broader view at the macro-economic or national economic impact of active labour market programmes, drawing on a small number of empirical studies from the US and the UK. In the US in the 1990s, the question whether policy changes *or* changes in the macro-economic climate played the larger role in shrinking the welfare caseload pre-occupied many academic and policy analysts, who developed different econometric models to explore the interactions between local or regional workfare programmes and macro-economic, national change. In the UK, there has been much less focus on this topic. To-date, there has been just one attempt to estimate the impact of the New Deal on the overall decline in unemployment among New Deal target groups. At the same time, it is clear that knowing how active labour market policies perform under changing economic conditions is essential to designing adaptable flexible programmes that retain their effectiveness as social and economic contexts change.

How Effective are Training Programmes?

The introduction of the New Deal in the UK was, to a large extent, driven by disillusionment with conventional job training and retraining programmes, which had been at the core of UK labour market policy in previous decades (cp. Chapter 3). Whereas training or retraining the jobless appeared appropriate at a time when jobseekers were a homogenous group of young unemployed people or unskilled and semi-skilled workers recently made redundant, changes in the structure of unemployment and the composition of the group of unemployed called the wisdom of human capital approaches to labour market policy into question. As unemployment continued to rise, the prevailing perception among policy analysts and policymakers was that, as a measure to improve employment prospects of the unemployed, skills training did not work, and the 'negative evidence' that emerged from training programme evaluations in the early 1980s appeared to confirm this view. At the same time, alternative evidence from both the US and, at a smaller scale, the UK suggested that active labour market policies, which placed a greater onus on the unemployed person's responsibility to obtain work and relied less on training, but more on job placements, would be promising alternatives, which could replace the outdated and largely ineffective system of passive labour market measures.

The Organisation for Economic Co-operation and Development (OECD) played an important role in reinforcing this perception. The findings of its Job Study (1994), to which national governments, including UK civil servants[33], contributed, were well received among UK policy makers, analysts and politician. It appeared to confirm the benefits of policies pursued by the Conservative government at the time and also matched the policy agenda of the in-coming Labour government. Later updates of the Job Study reiterated this point. Flexible working time, the easing of employment law, and the removal of 'employment security provisions that inhibit the expansion of employment in the private sector' (OECD, 1996, p. 15) were central tenets of the organisation's agenda of active labour market policies. It recommended that unemployment and related welfare benefits be reduced 'where they can be considered overly generous' (OECD, 1996, p. 25); that job search be enforced and that net incomes in work be increased through tax or benefit changes.

---

[33] The OECD Job Study brought together individual country reports submitted by national experts, who often were government civil servants, and often represented 'official' interpretations of fact and events. Making this point is not disputing *per se* the validity of the claims made in these national reports, as they may form a (self-) critical basis for cross-national comparisons. However, the method of compilation and their subsequent presentation entail the risk of self-fulfilling prophecy and self-referential circularity of argument, as was, in fact, apparent in the UK. The parts of the OECD study that pertained to Britain, in particular its praise for the UK efforts to reform labour market policy, were derived from material that more frequently resembled opinions or anecdote than evidence. The study was used, in turn, as justification for continuing the country's welfare-to-work reform programme (cp. Chapter 3).

The OECD report was critical of training programmes, although perhaps less so than was often assumed, particularly in government circles. In coming to its conclusions, the study drew a distinction between different types of job training schemes. It argued that evidence from the US shown that whilst 'large-scale training programmes in a class-room setting...have been particularly unsuccessful' (OECD, 1994, p. 27), some of the targeted training (and employment) programmes appeared to been fairly effective. Nonetheless, in its general conclusions, the study argued against more training schemes and, instead, pointed out that 'evaluations show that targeted measures of job-search assistance and counselling, as pioneered by the United Kingdom with its re-start interviews, back-to-work plans and job clubs, have a consistently positive impact on employment and earnings of participants' (ibid, p. 27). As a result of such evidence, the OECD came to advocate the integration of public employment services, including job placements, and the administration of unemployment benefits, again highlighting the UK as one country that was already taking steps towards achieving a more integrated system.

Not all reports that emerged from the offices of the OECD in the mid-1990s were as critical of training programmes for the unemployed as the Job Study had been. In 1996, a more nuanced review of active labour market measures reported that the most effective training programmes were well targeted and took place in small groups (Fay, 1996). This report built on evaluations of the UK Employment Training and Employment Action programmes (see 7.2) and the US JTPA-II-A programme.[34] Looking in more detail at training programmes, the study's author remarked that much of the effectiveness of training programme-based active labour market measures, in fact, depended on the quality of the training provided. Training and retraining jobseekers should, therefore, neither be summarily dismissed nor should they 'be used as a solution to large-scale unemployment' (Fay, 1996, p.18). They were unlikely to be effective means for combating high unemployment, but might still assist jobseekers' re-entry into local labour market through services customised to jobseekers' and employers' skill needs.

However, some analysts, including Fay, were concerned that the effectiveness of training programmes was undermined because they reduced or delayed job search activities among jobseekers who participated in them. As non-employment extended with the duration of the training programmes, this, in turn, adversely affected participants' re-employment.

Moreover, some programmes were felt to provide disincentives to search for a job even after this ended because they allowed participants to re-qualify for certain types of social security benefits after completing the training programme, entitlement for which they would otherwise have had exhausted. In such instances, training programmes risked failing to move trainees 'from welfare-to-work' by eliminating job search altogether.

---

[34] Job Training and Partnership Act Title II retraining programme, directed at adult economically disadvantaged people, including recipients of Aid for Families with Dependent Children (AFDC).

The effectiveness of labour market programmes, particularly training programmes that, in the UK, can extend over several months, if not years, is difficult to assess. Labour market initiative with long lead-in and support times also require long follow-up periods. This does usually not occur. Moreover, even training programmes of short duration are not necessarily expected to lead to instant result and require long periods of observation before showing effects. In the absence of *long-term* evaluation data of training programmes, a review or critique of training or retraining programmes, therefore, ought to be guarded (Meager with Evans, 1997). Training programmes can only be expected to show effects in the medium-term or long-term, but participants of programmes are hardly ever tracked over sufficient time to provide a robust assessment of the programmes' effectiveness.

Only recently have more long-term monitoring and survey data that are designed to track programme participants become available in the UK. In addition, labour market analyses seeking to investigate long-term trends can increasingly draw on secondary data, that is, data not specifically collected with a view to monitoring or evaluating the performance of training programmes. These data can typically be extracted from surveys, which were concerned not with training issues or labour market policy, but nevertheless collect relevant information. Such surveys include national panel and some birth cohort studies conducted in European countries, including the UK, as well as the US.

A recent review of labour market programme evaluations in Germany, Sweden, Denmark and The Netherlands assembled evaluation evidence from a series of studies using panel studies and other, more focussed longitudinal studies of labour market programmes (Rabe, 2000). Its review of the evidence contradicts the cautious note of Meager and Evans (1997) as it concluded that training programmes might not pay off even in the long term. It would appear that the increased employment probability that is undeniably derived from the increase in human capital due to participation in training programmes, typically does not compensate for the adverse effect of delayed job search. This is particularly likely if training courses are of long duration (12 months or more). One seemingly counter-intuitive reason for this may be that employers use participation in training programmes for jobseekers as a screening criterion to rule out rather than rule in job applicants if labour supply is sufficient (Rabe, 2000).

Labour Market Programmes in the UK

Studies in the UK have echoed some of the international research findings and have concluded that small-scale and well-targeted training programmes work best and that immediate placements in work prove most effective (Robinson, 2000). In this section, the findings from evaluations of some of the most prominent UK active labour market programmes of the 1990s (and indeed late 1980s) are reviewed. Prior to the New Deal, these programmes were critical in shaping the perception of policy analysts, policy makers and economic researchers concerning the need for a reform of labour market policy. Table 7.1 summarizes the key features of these programmes.

The aim of this review is not to provide a comprehensive account of all training and job search programmes implemented in the UK during or just before the 1990s. This would require a book in itself. The focus will instead be on some of the larger and more prominent national and national pilot programmes, which were immediate predecessors to the present-day New Deal programme or programmes and which have been independently evaluated.[35]

A brief history The UK's first national, mandatory 'activation' programme was Restart (Table 7.1). Introduced in the mid-1980s, its aim was to enforce active job search among claimants of active benefits by requiring them to attend interviews in social security offices to determine their need for job search activities and, in later meetings, to monitor these and to provide job search counselling. Although evaluations found that the programme was only moderately successful and were unclear as to which components of the programme (counselling, job-search assistance or the threat of benefit sanctions in case of non-compliance) proved most effective, the nature of the intervention nonetheless served as a model for future active labour market initiatives in the UK. Since Restart, advice and the monitoring of the job-search activities of benefit claimants have become core elements of most labour market programmes and have repeatedly been shown to be cost-effective means of reducing the claimant count and assisting jobseekers back into work.[36] Restart interviews were retained when Jobseekers Allowance replaced insurance-based income support and unemployment benefit in 1996, and claimants were called for interviews after 13 and 26 weeks of unemployment. In several of the New Deal programmes, restart interviews were replaced by the 'Gateway' interviews, while long-term claimants of Jobseeker's Allowance not participating in any of the New Deal programmes continue to be required to attend mandatory Restart advisory interviews after six and 12 months of unemployment. The interviews are followed by six-week programmes of 'intensive jobmatching', which involve increased and regular contact with JobCentre advisors.

Programmes that followed Restart were attempts at refining existing programmes; to design programmes for specific target groups, such as the young unemployed or lone parents; or to extract and retain elements of larger programmes, while parent programmes were discontinued. Some of these programmes have survived the introduction of the New Deal, while others became redundant as the New Deal offered similar and, sometimes, more comprehensive support of similar nature.

---

[35] Programmes targeted at special needs groups, such as Access to Work, which aims to help disabled workers, cannot be reviewed here. Other special targeted interventions that are not reviewed here include Job Review Workshops, which is targeted at unemployed individuals with professional, executive or managerial backgrounds, and *progress2work*, which is aimed at drug users.

[36] It is important to note that reducing the claimant count and assisting jobseekers into work are different programme outcome. It is apparent that many claimants were removed or removed themselves from the claimants register under the threat of sanction without ever attending a Restart or similar support programme.

Initially, however, programmes designed to train the unemployed went through phases of repeated modification. Employment Training (ET) and Employment Action (EA) were introduced in 1988 and 1991 respectively, providing on-the-job (ET) and off-the-job (EA) training for all long-term unemployed aged 18-50 and short-term unemployed young people (18-24). ET had itself replaced the New Job Training, which offered up to six months of work experience or training mainly to job seekers aged 18 to 25 years. Both ET and EA were merged into Training for Work (TfW) in 1993.

TfW no longer required participants to pursue a course leading to a National Vocational Qualification (NVQ) or equivalent, although most participants continued to do so (Sproston, 1999). In contrast, TfW emphasized assessment and guidance over direction and required that Action or Participation Plans be developed for each programme participant. The reason for doing away with the requirement for participants to pursue a qualification was largely to allow the programme deliverers, local Training and Enterprise Councils (TECs), greater flexibility in their training design. But TfW was also an attempt to move programme participants closer to the labour market. Unlike its predecessors, it allowed participants to enter a contract of employment with their placement providers. Regular wages, thus, replaced state-funded training allowances, while employers were offered subsidies to help with recruitment and the cost of training.

Simultaneous with TfW, the Community Action (CA) programme offered part-time work experience with voluntary and (local) community organisations, alongside job search assistance, for those individuals who had been unemployed for 12 or more months and preferred this option to TfW. In 1998, the TfW was replaced with Work-based Training (later: Learning) for Adults (WBTA/WBLA) programme. Two years prior to that, a new mandatory active labour market measure, Project Work (PW), had been introduced, absorbing the Workstart programme. At the same time, CA was wound up.

PW, albeit run only as a pilot scheme in a small number of local authorities, provided long-term unemployed people with 13 weeks of intensive job search training followed, where appropriate, by a 13-week mandatory work placement. A change in government and the introduction of the New Deal prevented a possible[37] national roll-out of PW, which was eventually itself wound up in 1998. However, Project Work's 13-week intensive job search component presented an important model for the structure and content of the New Deal Gateway that essentially replaced it.

---

[37] Possible, but not necessarily probable or indeed inevitable roll-out, because the previous Conservative Government had been concerned about the cost implications of PW's mandatory work placement element.

Table 7.1   UK Labour market programmes 1993-2000

Programme	Content	Participation/Target group	Period
Restart Interviews	Job counselling interviews after each 6 months of unemployment. 2-week Restart Course in job search skills after 24 month of Restart interviews..	Mandatory. Unemployed for 6 or more months.	1986- continuing
Employment Training	Off-the-job training and work placements (up to 1 year, later extended to up to 2 years).	Voluntary.	1988-1993
Employment Action	Placements with voluntary organisations (on average 6 months).	Voluntary.	1991-1993
Training for Work (replacing ET and EA)	Individual Action Plan or Participation Plan. Off-the-job training, employer placement, or project placement, or a combination of these.	Voluntary. 18-60 year olds unemployed for 6 or more months.	1993-1998
Community Action (CA)	Part-time work experiences on projects on benefit to the local community; job search assistance.	Voluntary. Unemployed for 12 months or more.	1993-1996
1-2-1	Up to six interviews with Job centre advisor as part of guided job search activity.	Mandatory. 18-24 year old unemployed 12 or more months. From April 1997, 2 or more years unemployed.	1994-1998 (replaced by Jobfinder Plus)

Table 7.1 continued

Programme	Content	Participation/Target group	Period
Work-Based Learning for Adults (replacing Work-Based Training for Adults, which in turn had replaced TfW)	Job-focussed and occupational training, self-employment support. Unemployed 6-12 months: up to 6 weeks training. Unemployed 12 months+: up to 12 months training.	Voluntary. 25-63 year old unemployed (6 months +).	1998-1999 (Work-Based Training for Adults) 1999 – continuing
WorkTrials	Up to 3 weeks of no-commitment placement with employer. Jobseekers continue to receive benefits, expenses.	Voluntary. 18 years of age or over. Unemployed for at least 6 months.	1993- continuing
Jobclubs	Job search, job preparation and presentation training; located in disadvantaged areas and town centres.	Voluntary; could last several months (no time limit). Jobseekers out of work for six or more months.	Piloted 1984; expansion and consolidation from 1986; continuing
Job Interview Guarantee	Interview with employer arranged by Employment Service for jobseeker.	Voluntary.	1989 –1999
Workstart	Employer subsidy of £60 per week (first six months) and £30 per week (second six months) for recruiting long-term unemployed.	Voluntary. Piloted in six areas between June 1993 and Mar 1996.	1993 – 1996 (absorbed into Project Work)
Project Work	13 weeks of intensive job search followed by 13 weeks of work placement.	Mandatory pilot scheme. 18-50 year old long-term unemployed (2 or more years).	1996-1998
New Deal for Young People (18-24 years)	Job search advice and monitoring with view to placing participants in paid job. Secondary Options.	Mandatory. 18-24 year old unemployed for six or more months.	1998 – continuing

Table 7.2 **Employment impacts by UK labour market programmes (in percentage points difference between programme and comparison/control group)**

Programme (author/s)	Evaluation Method	Evaluation Year	Observation Period	Employment Impact
Restart (White and Lakey, 1992)	Random control group/ experimental design	1989-90	1 year[1]	+ 1.8pp
			1.5 year	+ 4.2pp
Employment Training (Payne et al., 1996)	Matched comparison	1993	1 year[1]	+ 3 pp
			3 year[1]	+ 22pp
Employment Action (Payne et al., 1996)	Matched comparison	1993	1 year[1]	- 1pp
			3 year[1]	+ 4pp
Work Trial (White et al., 1997)	Matched comparison	1994/95	0.5 year	+ 34pp
Jobclub (White et al., 1997)	Matched comparison	1995	0.5 year	+ 6pp
Job Interview Guarantee (White et al., 1997)	Matched comparison	1995	0.5 year	+ 11pp
Training for Work (Payne et al., 1999)	Matched comparison	1996-97	1 year[1]	-/-
			2 years[1]	+6pp
			3 years[1]	+12pp
			4 years[1]	+14pp
1-2-1 (Boutall and Knight, 1998)	Random assignment across sample of 15 ES offices	May 1996 – March 1997	0.5 years (after Restart interview)	+6pp

Table 7.2 continued

Programme (author/s)	Evaluation Method	Evaluation Year	Observation Period	Employment Impact
Project Work (Bryson et al., 1998)[2]	Matched area comparison	1996/97	50 weeks[1]	+ 4.3pp
Work-based Learning for Adults (Anderson et a., 2003)	Propensity score matching	2003	12–15 months	SJFT[4] -/- LOT[4] 7pp BET[4] -/-
New Deal for Long-Term Unemployed Pilots (Lissenburgh, 2001)	Propensity score matching	Dec 1998–Feb 1999	4-6 months / 10–12 months / 16–18 months / 22–24 months	+11.7pp / +11.8pp / +4.5pp / +2.9pp
New Deal for Young People[3] (Riley and Young, 2000, p.32, Table 2.5)	Difference-in-difference (econometric modelling)	1999 (quarter 1) / 2000 (quarter 1)	April 1998–April 1999 / April 1998–April 2000	+ 13,000 / + 16,000

Note: Evaluation Year refers to the start or sampling period of the evaluation. Observation Period is the period over which impacts were measured. Employment Impact (in percentage points, pp), is the difference between the employment change (in %) experienced by programme participants and by non-participants over the given period. No difference is indicated by -/-.
[1] From start of prior (qualifying) spell of unemployment; otherwise from entry to programme.
[2] This estimate is calculated for only one of the pilot areas (Medway/Maidstone).
[3] Benchmark groups for Difference-in-Difference approach: 25-29 and 30-49 year old unemployed. Impacts exclude government supported trainees; in 000s.
[4] SJFT – Short Job Focussed Training, LOT – Longer Occupational Training, BET – Basic Employability Training

Apart from WBTA/WBLA, just two active labour market programmes of the 1990s survive to the present day, while another (1-2-1) was again replaced by a new programme of essentially similar content (Jobfinder Plus[38]). One of the two surviving programmes is the Work Trials programme, which offers up to three weeks of work placements with employers, without committing the jobseeker or the employer to enter into a contractual employment arrangement after the placement. The other programme consists of Jobclubs, which offer walk-in facilities around the country with access to job search and job preparation training, tools and technology.

Programme Evaluations

The training, placement and job search programmes described in the previous section have been subject to evaluations of their effects on the number or proportion of programme participants taking up paid work. In this section, findings from these evaluations are reported and compared, focussing on employment (Table 7.2). The choice of impact indicator in this section is very much driven by their use in the evaluations. Most evaluations – and all of the schemes included in this comparison – measure and report programme impacts on the employment of participants. Some, but not all, also include estimates of the programmes' effects on participants' receipt of social security benefits. One study also tried to measure impacts on incomes and, unusual for this type of analysis, workplace productivity (Anderson et al., 2003).

Even when limiting estimated programme impacts to those on employment, it is important to acknowledge some of the caveats. This is because the evaluations used variable definitions of the outcome 'employment', which could include any employment, full-time or full-time equivalent employment, self-employment, subsidized or unsubsidized employment, etc. Unfortunately, some studies are insufficiently clear about the definitions they used and it was not possible to standardize the employment impact indicator. Moreover, the studies varied in the length of the evaluation periods that they used. Five of the twelve programmes listed in Table 7.2 considered the observation period of the evaluation to commence with the start of the spell of unemployment that qualified programme participants for programme entry. This invariably increases the window of observation, although the persons observed might not have been on the programme for all of that time. Other evaluations viewed the observation window as the one starting with entry onto a programme. Allowance should be made for such cases, which would be expected to show less evidence of impact.

Finally, the job training and placement programmes operated in different locations, under variable social and economic conditions, and targeted somewhat

---

[38] Jobfinder Plus provides mandatory job-focussed interviews for unemployed people aged 25 or over who have been out of work for 18 or more months. A similar service is provided for the same target group by the New Deal for Unemployed People (ND25+). Jobfinder Plus is often perceived as a tool for facilitating the transition onto ND25+; it is not available to individuals already participating in ND25+.

different client groups. Bar conducting another meta-analysis, which is not the objective here, it is impossible to control for these variations, which naturally affects their success. The transferability of evaluation results from one location to another, or from one time (and economic climate) to another, from one client group to another, therefore, cannot be assumed.

The programmes brought together in this review have been evaluated using a range of evaluation techniques, which included random designs (random assignment design), propensity score matching, matched comparison, including matched area comparisons, and econometric modelling based on a difference-in-difference approach. These are among the most stringent evaluation methods available, although none can be said to be entirely infallible and not subject to technically or methodological error. In fact, at least one of the studies, the evaluation of Project Work, encountered substantial problems in the course of the evaluation as a result of low response rates in the follow-up survey of programme participants and gaps and inconsistencies in the administrative data used to assess programme impacts (Bryson et al., 1988). The findings from this study should, therefore, be treated with caution, although they are included in this review.

Bearing these caveats in mind, the following general conclusions can be drawn from comparing the job training and placement programme evaluations in Table 7.3:

- In most instances, employment impacts have been fairly small, but positive. Only the Employment Action (EA) programme, evaluated in 1993, showed a negative impact in the first year, when proportionately fewer programme participants entered employment than non-participants in the control areas. However, this negative impact was reversed after three years when four percentage points more programme participants than non-participants entered employment.
- A small number of programmes were found to have performed rather well. The Employment Training (ET), Work Trial (WT), Job Interview Guarantee (JIG), Training for Work (TfW) programmes all achieved a 'double-digit' employment impact, although in the case of ET and TfW this was not achieved until three years into the observation period. WT and JIG, in contrast, reported these high impacts after just six months.
- Programmes, for which repeated impact measurements are available, apparently improved over time. Thus, the impact of ET increased from three percentage points in Year 1 to 22 percentage points in Year 3. The impact of Restart increased from under two percentage points to just over four percentage points in the relative short interval between the first 12 and 18 months of the evaluation period. The Employment Action (EA) programme also recorded an employment impact of four percentage points after three years, following a negative impact in its first year. TfW's impacts also increased, especially between its second (6pp) and third year (12pp).

- The impacts of training programmes were monitored for longer periods than those of job counselling and advice services, and, over these periods, recorded among the highest impacts.
- Only one of the evaluated programmes sought to increase the employability of participants through 'preparation for work' in the voluntary sector rather than the private sector (Employment Action, EA). Compared to other employer-focussed programmes, in particular its 'twin' Employment Training, EA had much smaller employment impacts.
- More recent evaluation evidence from the WBLA programme appears to contradict some earlier evidence by suggesting that longer, intensive occupational training may be more effective than short job-focussed training, which may last up to six weeks, and also more effective than training in basic employment skills, which typically lasts up to 26 weeks.
- Finally, after one year of monitoring participants, the employment impact of the New Deal for the Long-term Unemployed was broadly similar to that of previous employment placement and activation programmes. The five percentage point increase in employment rates among participants in this programme was higher than that achieved by Restart after the same period (1.8 percentage points), but slightly lower than that achieved by Jobclubs (six percentage points), which have features that are also included in the New Deal. No comparable data are available from Riley and Young's evaluation (2000) of the New Deal for Young People, although their calculations increase in employment among young people of 13,000 to 16,000 as a result of the New Deal. This would be equivalent to an extra 0.5 per cent of young people in employment in the year 2000.

The evaluation findings listed above support the key arguments that have accompanied the transition, in recent years, towards more active labour market policy. As discussed earlier, these arguments include that work placements should receive greater emphasis than training schemes. However, on the basis of above evidence, it would be wrong to dismiss training programmes categorically as ineffective and incapable of helping people to move into employment. Training programmes have, in fact, been able to improve the employment prospects of participants, but they tend to take comparatively more time to achieve placements and do so for fewer people.

A similar point has been made with respect to the UK New Deal for Young People. The Voluntary Sector Option and Environment Task Force component of this programme have proved less effective in ensuring that participants progress into unsubsidized employment outside the New Deal than has the Employment Option (comprising of subsidized work) (Bonjour et al., 2001). Moreover, the intensive job search Gateway component, which is similar in approach to Jobclubs and the Job Interview Guarantee programme, has been effective in channelling job seekers into work (Blundell et al., 2001; Dorsett, 2001).

Because job training programmes take longer to implement, operate and achieve their outcomes, they are more costly than most job-focussed programmes. Evidence reported by Fay and Rabe suggests that costs can be reduced and effectiveness increased by fine-tuning these programmes and delivering them as short specialist courses. However, in the UK, the evaluation of Work-Based Learning for Adults suggested that, by contrast, longer occupational training courses could be relatively more successful than shorter work place-focussed or employability courses. In the light of this somewhat contradictory evidence, more and more detailed research will be required to ascertain the best approach to providing effective training programmes.

US Training Programmes

The finding from UK evaluation that job search and placement programmes produce better outcomes than job training programmes, of course, resonates with the US experience and the findings of the meta-analysis reported in the previous chapters. While several studies have reflected on the effectiveness of training programmes in the US, the findings of just three are reported here. These three are of interest because of their comparative nature and the conclusions they draw from their analyses.

The earliest of the three studies was prepared and published in the late 1990s by Heckman, LaLonde and Smith (Heckman et al., 1999). Although primarily a theoretical review of the methodology of labour market policy evaluation, Heckman et al. also summarize the evaluation findings of prominent US labour market programmes. Relying above all on evaluations and impact estimations of the National JTPA (Job Training Partnership Act) programme (implemented between 1983 and 1998) and the National Supported Work (NSW) Demonstration (1975-1978), the authors found little evidence to suggest that training programmes helped to raise the earnings of programme participants. However, there were exceptions, such as JTPA, which proved to be highly effective programmes, albeit mainly for women:

> Indeed, for economically disadvantaged adult women residing in the US, a case can be made that these programs consistently have been a productive social investment, whose returns are larger than those from schooling. For other groups this conclusion clearly does not hold (Heckman et al., 1999, p.2054).

The authors found the same to be true for their review of some 20 employment and training programmes, which had been evaluated using social experiments.[39]

---

[39] The discussion by Heckman et al. (1999) of social experiments covered many evaluations also included in our meta-analysis, such as GAIN, Minnesota MFIP and San Diego SWIM (see Chapter 4), as well as others, which did not meet out selection criteria, such as Maine TOPS, Food Stamps Employment & Training Programme. Our meta-analysis was concerned with AFDC programmes only and, for this reason, excluded the Food Stamps

Heckman et al. again stress the effectiveness of such programmes for adult women, but also point out that, while job search assistance 'appears to be the most cost-effective service [...], more expensive WE (work experience, AC) and training programs result in larger absolute earnings gains' (Heckman et al., 1999, p. 2055). They come to the same conclusion for adult males, arguing that 'the evidence suggests that programs that offer training can raise the earnings of economically disadvantaged adult males, but programs that focus on JSA (job search activity, AC) or WE appear to be ineffective or sometimes worse' (Heckman, et al., 1999, pp. 2055-56).

In most instances, low-skilled participants appeared least likely to benefit from welfare-to-work programmes, although some programmes produced larger than average gains. Perhaps counter-intuitively, given the relative effectiveness of training measures just noted, the programmes most likely to help the least skilled were programmes, which included work experience as an important part of their services, rather than emphasising training. In summary, therefore, Heckman et al's review showed that training programmes were able to improve the earnings and employment potential, in particular, of adult women, but work experience was more effective for low-skilled jobseekers.

In the mid-1990s, the second of the three studies highlighted here was published. This review of experimental and quasi-experimental evaluations of training programmes was produced by Rob Fisher (Fisher, 1995) and was more comprehensive, in terms of the number of evaluations that were covered, than the one produced by Heckman and his colleagues. In total, Fisher reviewed 65 voluntary and mandatory programmes implemented between 1973 and 1993, including programmes, which used a mix of human capital development and job search techniques, recording and comparing their impacts over four consecutive quarters. For most programmes, Fisher found that the reported impacts were small, yet typically statistically significant. By the fourth quarter, participants in these training programmes had experienced, on average, a three-percentage point increase in their employment rate (33 per cent among the experimental groups, 30 per cent among the control groups). At the same time, the proportion of programme participants who were in receipt of AFDC was 71 per cent compared to 73 per cent of the control groups.

Among the diverse range of programmes he examines, Fisher noted that, over the four-quarter period, job search interventions showed early positive impacts on employment, whereas basic education programs initially showed negative effects, although these impacts gradually increased, as did those for vocational training and on-the-job training programmes. Fisher's conclusions, in fact, echoed those of the international comparative studies reported earlier in this chapter, which suggested that while training programmes – almost inevitably – have negative impacts in the short term, in the longer term they are capable of producing positive outcomes.

---

programmes. Maine's Training Opportunities in the Private Sector (TOPS) programme was omitted because it was open only to applicants rather than mandatory for all AFDC recipients.

Whereas Fisher's study was based on a comparison of evaluations, more recently, Greenberg et al. (2003) undertook a meta-analysis of training programmes, most of which combined a mix of on-the-job training and classroom-based vocational or skills training with job search, remedial education, or subsidized employment in private and public sectors. The authors sought to identify the type of training that offered the best employment prospects from programme participants, although they were not concerned to determine whether training programmes were more effective than work-placements or work-first approaches. Their synthesis included 31 evaluations of 15 voluntary training programmes, which were operated in the US between 1964 and 1988. The earliest programme in their sample was launched with the Manpower Development and Training Act (MDTA), a national programme, which was aimed at disadvantaged adults and youth and was implemented between 1962-1973. The most recent was the national training programme initiated under the Job Training Partnership Act (JTPA), a national programme, which commenced in 1983 and was run until 1998 when it was replaced by a similar programme. The evaluations covered both national and regional programmes and used a range of evaluation methods, not just random assignment techniques.

Focussing on the earnings impact of training programmes, Greenberg et al.'s analyses found significant differences between the impacts for men, women and young people. In general, training programmes appeared to work best for adult women, but the effectiveness of these programmes in improving the earnings of adult men was at best small. However, even for adult women, the size of the impacts was modest. Classroom-based skills training appeared to have been most effective, except for basic education. Numerous variations in effectiveness among different participant groups and in different socio-economic conditions were apparent.

Yet, the study's most crucial finding was that, despite more than 30 years of implementing and experimenting with different types of training programmes, there was, in fact, no evidence that these programmes had become more effective over time. In spite of a long history of effort, it appeared that the implementation of training programmes had yet to be perfected or that training programmes were destined to produce limited returns. Importantly, more capital-intensive programmes were not necessarily more effective either, although there was some evidence that young people benefited more from more expensive programmes.

Another Perspective: Focus on Costs

All three studies, therefore, agree that US training programmes have had positive impacts, but primarily for women, and that frequently these impacts have been small. The limited return that training programmes offer is a major concern of many critics of active labour market policy in the US and, increasingly, also in the UK. Given their small returns, Heckman (1998) has criticized US training programmes for the low-skilled jobseekers for being, in his view, unreasonably costly. His main argument rests on an analysis of changes in earnings inequality in the US, the reduction of which he perceives as a key performance indicator of social and economic policy.

Heckman points out that, between 1979 and 1989, the real earnings of male high-school drop-outs and high-school graduates declined by 13 per cent and four per cent respectively, and estimated that some $426 billion in 1989 dollars would be required in human capital investment in order to restore the earnings of these males to their real levels in 1979. Reversing the widening earnings gap would require an additional $1,152 billion in 1989 dollars. The costs would rise even further, if this were attempted for female high-school drop-outs and graduates.

He contrasts these estimates with a review of 13 training programme evaluations, which he concludes have shown only small impacts. Since even mandatory programmes 'produce little long-term gain' (Heckman, 1998, p. 112), Heckman argues that further investment in such programmes, in particular where they primarily attempt to assist low-skilled individuals, is economically unwarranted. Instead, it would be economically more efficient to invest in the post-school training of higher-skilled workers, and he recommends that training should focus on this group of workers and that 'the tax system [should be used] to transfer resources to the less-skilled through wage subsidies ...' (Heckman, 1998, p.116).

From an economic point of view, Heckman's suggestion is intuitive and appears to offer an answer to the protracted problem of efficiency in resource allocation in social and economic policy. In fact, within the New Deal for Young People, subsidized employment, the first of the four Options, has proven comparatively more successful in guiding young people into unsubsidized work than any of the other Options (Bonjour et al., 2001). The evidence for the US also suggests that subsidies have a positive impact on employment rates (Katz, 1996; cited in White and Knight, 2002). However, Heckman's scheme is not without flaws. It appears to overlook the social implications and the likely social costs of what is proposed. Abandoning to the training of those with fewer skills will almost inevitably reduce social and occupational mobility. In turn, this is likely to lead to a further segmentation of the labour market, causing itself inefficiencies in the demand and supply of labour.

National Impact Analyses of Welfare-to-Work Programmes

Heckman's reflections on the cost efficiency of job training programmes lead naturally to a recurrent issue among observers of welfare-to-work programmes, namely, the contribution of welfare-to-work programmes to the decline in welfare caseloads in the US. One issue within the US debate about the benefits and costs of welfare-to-work programmes has been the question whether it was national economic forces, rather than the programmes that caused the recorded decline in welfare caseloads.

Leaving aside descriptive studies, which have merely – and rather simplistically – mapped changes in caseloads and asserted that these changes are attributable to expenditure on welfare-to-work programmes or the extent to which programmes used sanctions (e.g. Rector and Youssef, 1999), three studies stand out that have used more complex econometrical modelling exercizes to determine the interaction between caseloads on the one hand and welfare reform programmes and macro-economic change on the other. The three have produced different results.

The first study, conducted by the Council of Economic Advisers (CEA), reviewed caseload changes between January 1993 and January 1997, when the number of claimants of AFDC declined by 20 per cent or 2.75m (CEA, 1997). The CEA estimated that about 40 per cent of the decline was due to falling unemployment associated with economic expansion and that 31 per cent of the decline resulted from the introduction of statewide welfare reform waivers, which led to the introduction of welfare-to-work programmes across the US. The remaining quarter of the decline was estimated to have been due to other, unspecified factors. Among others, this study controlled for different types of waivers granted to the states, the substantial increase in the generosity of the Earned Income Tax Credit, and the industrial composition of US States' economy. In addition, the model included state-specific time trend variables designed to control for fixed effects.

In 1999, the CEA updated its analysis, this time covering the period from 1996 to 1998, during which the national caseload fell by one third (CEA, 1999). The slightly revised econometric model estimated that 35 per cent to 45 per cent of caseload decline between 1996 and 1998 was due to the effect of the *time-limited* TANF, which had replaced AFDC by that time, and that eight per cent to ten per cent of the decline had been due to general economic improvements and the associated decline in unemployment.[40]

Over time, therefore, the CEA evidence suggested an increased relative effectiveness of welfare reforms over that of macro-economic factors, although the modifications undertaken to the model in the second analysis make a direct comparison impossible. The impact of model specifications on the results of econometric analysis was the main issue raised by Figlio and Ziliak (1999) in their review of the caseload literature in the US. The authors had previously estimated that improved economic conditions had accounted for nearly two-thirds of the decline in caseloads, while welfare reforms were found to have had no significant impact (Ziliak et al., 1997). This point was reiterated in their attempt at reconciling different estimating methods.

Unlike CEA, which used the absolute number of AFDC recipients as the basis for their analysis, Figlio and Ziliak used AFDC caseloads *per capita* as their dependent variable. Moreover, Ziliak et al's original model differed substantially

---

[40] The study also sought to account for the effect of the minimum wage and for changes in the level of cash benefits granted by states. The minimum wage, which was increased during this phase, was estimated to have accounted for between ten and 16 per cent of the decline in caseloads, while lower cash benefits were calculated to have accounted for between one and five per cent of the decline.

from the CEA's as well as from those used in other studies – for example, Blank (1998) or Moffitt (1987) – in two other respects. First, it used monthly rather than annual state-level caseload data, which gave the model a greater dynamic. Second, the authors included a number of time lags in their model. These variables were used to estimate and control for state dependence, business cycles and the lag in implementing welfare waivers. Figlio and Ziliak concluded that caseloads were slow to respond to changes in unemployment rates, but that macro-economic change ultimately accounted for 75 per cent of the decline in AFDC recipient rates between 1993 and 1996. Welfare reform, on the other hand, was estimated to have had a negative impact, retarding the decline in caseloads by 2.5 per cent.

There have so far been no comparable attempts to measure the macro-economic impact of welfare-to-work programmes in the UK, although the National Institute for Social and Economic Research (NISER), commissioned by the Employment Service (reported in NAO, 2002), estimated the New Deal for Young People's (NDYP) net contribution to youth employment and to (reduced) unemployment among young people. It concluded that due to the NDYP in its first two years of operation until March 2000, more than 20,000 young people left unemployment sooner than they otherwise would have. After taking account of the dynamics of youth labour market flows into and out of unemployment, youth unemployment was estimated to have fallen by 35,000 and youth employment had risen by 15,000 as a result of the New Deal (see also Table 7.2).[41] According to the ONS Labour Force Survey, between summer 1998 and summer 2000, employment among 18 to 24 year olds increased by approximately 39,000, from 3,308m to 3,3,47m. NISER's estimate suggests that about 40 per cent of this increase in youth employment was due to the New Deal for Young People.

Conclusion

A view widely held among policymakers, policy analysts and politicians in the UK in the mid- and late-1990s was that training programmes were failing to help their participants obtain employment. In this chapter, it was argued that this view only partially reflected evaluation evidence. However, much of this evidence was still being gathered and several important studies only emerged towards the end of that decade. In the end, the evidence suggested that training programmes did not always fail or prove ineffective when compared to work placement or job counselling services, and were, in fact, able to help participants into paid work. However, they typically took longer to achieve a similar level of effectiveness as work placement programmes. Analysts have argued that whether a training programme succeeded or not frequently depended on the quality of training that was provided, and its intensity. Short courses appeared to work better than long

---

[41] Allowing for secondary effects of increased job search activity and increased job placement of long-term unemployed youth, NISER estimated that employment among people outside the NDYP target group of 18-24 year olds had increased by about 10,000.

courses, which reduced participants' attachment to the labour market while they were undergoing training. But there is little systematic analysis of the differential effectiveness of different types of training courses. Moreover, a recent evaluation of Work-Based Training for Adults also found positive impacts for longer training courses.

The advantage of programmes that focus work placement rather than training (e.g. *Work-First* programmes) has been their greater flexibility and lower costs. Training programmes are more costly to operate, in particular when managed by public sector bodies, which must pay for premises and training staff (see Chapter 1 for New Deal costs). Work placement programmes transfer these costs to employees, albeit at the risk of low-skilled, low-income individuals not receiving any or much training at all.

Work-First programmes also transfer the decision as to who to train and what skills to train them in to the employer. Whereas this could conceivable raise issues of social equity and social justice, Heckman (1998) has argued that *not* training the low skilled would make economic sense. In the long term, however, this strategy could undermine economic as well as social objectives, particularly if it was to curtail improvements in national productivity through a better-qualified workforce (Haskel and Pereira, 2002).

Finally, the extent to which welfare-to-work programmes have produced net benefits to national economies remains disputed in the US, while there have been few attempt to estimate these benefits in the UK. For the US, the findings of the meta-analysis presented in this book suggest a positive impact of welfare-to-work programmes on caseloads (Chapter 4). However, this impact appears to be small. Moreover, the meta-analysis has shown that impacts diminish over time (Chapter 6). Thus, the measurement of the size of an intervention's impact on welfare caseloads may, ultimately, depend on how long after participants have entered a programme that measurement of the programme impact takes place.

References

Anderson, T., Dorsett, R., Hales, J., Lissenburgh, S., Pires, C., Smeaton, D. (2003), *Work-Based Learning for Adults: an evaluation of labour market effects*, Department for Work and Pensions, London.

Blank, R. (1998), *What Causes Public Assistance Caseloads to Grow?*, Working Paper No. 2, Joint Center for Poverty Research, Chicago.

Bloom, H.S., Hill, C. J., and Riccio, J. (2001), *Modeling the Performance of Welfare-to-Work Programs: The effects of program management and services, economic environment, and client characteristics*, MDRC, New York.

Blundell, R., Costa Dias, M., Meghir, C., and v. Reenan, J. (2001), *Evaluating the employment impact of a mandatory job search assistance program*, Working Paper WP01/20, Institute for Fiscal Studies, London.

Bonjour, D., Dorsett, R., Knight, G., Lissenburgh, S., Makherjee, A., Payne, J., Range, M., Urwin, P.,and White, M. (2001), *New Deal for Young*

People: National Survey of Participants: Stage 2, Research & Development Report ESR67, Employment Service, Sheffield.

Boutall, S. and Knight, M.A. (1998), *Evaluation of 1-2-1 for the Very Long Term Unemployed. Tracking Study*, Employment Service RED 115, Employment Service, Sheffield.

Bryson, A., Lissenburgh, S. and Payne, J. (1998), *The First Project Work Pilots: A quantitative evaluation*, Report to the Employment Service and the Department for Education and Employment, Policy Studies Institute, London.

Dorsett, R. (2001), *The New Deal for Young People: relative effectiveness of the options in reducing male unemployment*, Research Discussion Paper No. 7, Policy Studies Institute, London.

Fay, R.G. (1996), *Enhancing the effectiveness of active labour market policies: evidence from programme evaluations in OECD countries*, OECD Labour Market and Social Policy Occasional Papers No. 18, OECD, Paris.

Figlio, D.N. and Ziliak, J.P. (1999), 'Welfare reform, the business cycle, and the decline in AFDC caseloads' in S.H. Danzinger (ed.) *Economic Conditions and Welfare Reform*, W.E. Upjohn Institute for Employment Research, Kalamazoo/Michigan.

Fischer, R. (1995), *Job Training as a Means to 'Ending Welfare As we Know It': A Meta-Analysis of U.S. Welfare Employment Program Effects, Research Summary*, Vanderbilt University, Nashville/Tennessee.

Greenberg, D., Michalopoulos, C. and Robins, P.K. (2003), 'A Meta-Analysis of Government Sponsored Training Programs', *Industrial & Labor Relations Review*, vol. 57.1, pp. 31-53.

Hamilton, G., Freedman, S., Gennetian, L., Michalopoulos, C., Walter, J., Adans-Ciardullo, D., Gassman-Pines, A., McGroder, S., Zaslow, M., Ahluwalia, S., Brooks, J. with Small, E. and Ricchetti, B. (2001), *National Evaluation of Welfare-to-Work Strategies: How effective are different welfare-to-work approaches? Five-year adult and child impacts for eleven programs*, MDRC, New York.

Haskel, J. and Pereira, S. (2002) Skills and productivity in the UK using matched establishment and worker data, Office for National Statistics, London, www.statistics.gov.uk/articles/nojournal/Paper_6_skills_productivity.pdf; downloaded 26 June 2004.

Heckman, J. (1998) 'What should be our human capital investment policy?' *Fiscal Studies*, vol. 19.2, pp. 103-119.

Heckman, J.J., LaLonde,R.J., and Smith, J.A. (1999) 'The Economics and Econometrics of Active Labor Market Programs' in A. Ashenfelder and D. Card (eds.) Handbook of Labor Economics, Vol. 3., Elsevier Science, Amsterdam/New York, pp. 1865-2097.

Katz, L. (1996), *Wage Subsidies for the Disadvantaged*, NER Working Paper 5679, National Bureau of Economic Research, Cambridge, Ma.

Lissenburgh, S. (2001), *New Deal for the Long Term Unemployed Pilots: quantitative evaluation using stage 2 survey*, ESR81, Employment Service, Sheffield.

Mead, L. M. (1996), *Are welfare employment programs effective?*, Discussion Paper No. 1096-96, Institute for Research on Poverty, Wisconsin.

Meager, N. with Evans, C. (1997), *The evaluation of active labour market measures for the long-term unemployed*, International Labour Office, Geneva.

Moffitt, R. (1987), 'Historical Growth in Participation in Aid to Families with dependent Children: Was there a Structural Shift?', *Journal of Post-Keynesian Economics,* vol. 9.3, pp. 347-363.

NAO (2002), *The New Deal for Young People. Report by the Comptroller and Auditor General*, The Stationery Office, London.

OECD (1996), *The OECD Jobs Study: Implementing the Strategy*, OECD, Paris.

Payne, J., Lissenburgh, S., White, M. and Payne, C. (1996), *Employment Training and Employment Action: an evaluation by the matched comparison method*, Research Series No. 74, Department for Education and Employment, London.

Payne, J., Payne, C., Lissenburgh, S. and Range, M. (1999), *Work-based Training and Job Prospects for the Unemployed: An evaluation of Training for Work*, DfEE Research Report RR96, DfEE Publications, Sudbury.

Rabe, B (2000), *Wirkungen aktiver Arbeitsmarktpolitik. Evaluierungsergebnisse für Deutschland, Schweden, Dänemark und die Niederlande*, Discussion Paper FS 1 00-208, Wissenschaftszentrum Berlin für Sozialforschung, Berlin.

Rector, R.E. and Youssef, S.E. (1999) *The Determinants of Welfare Caseload Decline*, The Heritage Foundation, Washington.

Riley, R. and Young, G. (2000), *The New Deal for Young People: Implications for Employment and the Public Finances*, ESR62, Employment Service, Sheffield.

Robinson, P. (2000), 'Active labour-market policies: a case of evidence-based policy-making?', *Oxford Review of Economic Policy*, vol. 16.1, pp. 13-26.

Sproston, K (1999), *TfW: A survey of ex-participants. A report prepared for the Department for Education and Employment*, National Centre for Social Research, London.

Walker, R. (1991), *Thinking about Workfare: Evidence from the USA*, HMSO, London.

White, M. and Knight, G. (2002), *Benchmarking the effectiveness of NDYP. A review of European and US literature on the microeconomic effects of labour market programmes for young people*, paper submitted to PSI Discussion Paper (August), Policy Studies Institute, London.

White, M. and Lakey, J. (1992), *The Restart Effect: evaluation of a labour market programme for unemployed people*, London, Policy Studies Institute.

White, M., Lissenburgh, S. and Bryson, A. (1997), *The Impact of Public Job Placing Programmes*, Policy Studies Institute, London.

Ziliak, J.P., Figlio, D.N. Davis, E.E. and Connolly, L.S. (1997), *Accounting for the Decline in AFDC Caseloads: Welfare Reform or Economic Growth?*, Discussion paper no. 1151-97, Institute for Research on Poverty, Wisconsin-Madison.

Chapter 8

Lessons for Welfare Policy and Research

Andreas Cebulla and David Greenberg

This final chapter draws together the main findings from the meta-analyses reported in earlier chapters and reflects on the process of policy learning that accompanied the introduction of the New Deal programme in the UK.

The meta-analysis has provided valuable insights into the working of welfare-to-work programmes in the US, which have yet to be confirmed or rejected in similar studies for active labour market programmes in the UK. While commonly used in medical research, meta-analysis continues to be rarely applied in policy evaluation in the UK, although the increasing profile of the Campbell Collaboration has helped to promote meta-analysis in areas such as criminology and education. In social welfare policy, however, meta-analysis has yet to develop a substantive presence. In this chapter, some of the obstacles to extending the use of meta-analysis in social policy and welfare research will be explored and we suggest ways of helping meta-analysis to become a more widely used, effective tool for policy evaluation.

A second key theme of this book – in fact, the theme first addressed in this chapter – has been the evolution of the New Deal welfare-to-work programme in the UK. The New Deal marked a turning point in active labour market policy – at least, if one was to believe the hype that accompanied its implementation. Yet, as Chapters 1 and 2 have shown, the New Deal was not an entirely new concept and its introduction was more a re-arranging of policy measures than a revolution in design and delivery. Nowhere was this more apparent than in the context, in which the policy took shape. The New Deal resembles – and, in fact, is the result of – a complex concatenation of insights, ideas, research interpretation and political preferences. The extent to which the New Deal was also the product of policy learning, in particular, cross-Atlantic policy learning, has been one of the key questions we have sought to answer in this book. The present chapter will reflect on the aggregate evidence from meta-analysis of the US welfare-to-work evaluations and the retrospective study of the policy process leading up to the launch of the New Deal. At its heart lies the question: has meta-analysis added to our understanding of 'what works' in welfare-to-work programmes or had UK policymakers, in fact, already learned the 'right' lessons from their own, typically less systematic study of US programmes.

The chapter continues with a summary of the key findings of the meta-analysis before recalling the principal conclusions from our study of the process of policy-making and policy learning in the course of the design and implementation of the New Deal. The final section presents the main conclusions of this book.

Key Lessons from the Meta-Analysis

The last two decades or more have witnessed a paradigmatic shift in political attitudes towards the receipt of social security benefits in both the UK and the US, particularly the belief that benefit receipt should be conditional on active search for paid work or participation in job training programmes. In both countries, governments have responded by introducing, or facilitating the introduction of, welfare-to-work programmes. This book has presented the results of the first programme level, systematic meta-analysis or meta-evaluation of mandatory welfare-to-work programmes in the US.[42]

The analysis was made possible by the assembly of a unique database of 24 welfare-to-work programmes that were implemented across the US between 1982 and 1996 in over 50 locations. The database contains detailed information from evaluation reports about programme impacts, service provided by the evaluated programmes, and participants' characteristics. Uniquely, the database also incorporates social and economic data that describe the socio-economic conditions prevailing at the time of the programmes' implementation and evaluation. To our knowledge, this is the first time that a database has integrated longitudinal impact and programme-specific evaluation data and concurrent contextual information.

It is often said that the effects of US welfare-to-work programmes are generally positive but modest in magnitude. Our meta-analysis demonstrated the truth of this assertion (Chapter 4). For example, during the first two or three years after random assignment, a typical welfare-to-work programme that is included in our database increased earnings by less than $400 a year (in year 2000 dollars) and caused the receipt of AFDC to fall by around two percentage point during a calendar quarter. However, these effects varied greatly and there were some programmes – for example, those in Riverside and Portland – for which they were much larger.

As discussed in Chapter 5 and 6, the effects of welfare-to-work programmes *eventually* decline, but take some time to do so (Chapters 5 and 6). For example, the earnings effects of a typical welfare-to-work programme, while modest, first grow for nearly three years. After this period, however, the earnings of individuals assigned to the programme group began to converge with those of controls and after five or six years, the difference between the two groups erodes completely. A similar pattern exists for AFDC receipt.

---

[42] A study of voluntary programmes has been conducted by one of the authors and others (Greenberg et al., 2003) and Bloom, Hill, and Riccio, (2003) have provided a multi-level statistical synthesis of a smaller number of welfare-to-work evaluations using both individual level and aggregate data.

One rationale for assembling the database and conducting the subsequent meta-evaluation was because US policy developments are increasingly influencing policy-making in the UK. In particular, US welfare-to-work programmes have been taken as models of successful social intervention. Many policy analysts and policy makers in the UK (as well as the US) now hold the view that work-first approaches are the most effective strategies for reducing welfare dependency and, consequently, advocate mandatory work-first approaches for the UK (Field, 1995; HM Treasury, 1997, 2000). Work-first approaches stress moving benefit recipients into paid work rather than onto training or education courses, whenever possible. Chapter 6 explored the evidence base for the claim of their greater effectiveness.

For many years, views as to the merits of particular welfare-to-work approaches have been formed on the basis of the evidence provided by individual, and perhaps isolated, evaluations and case studies. The present meta-analysis is the first comprehensive review of the evidence available from the most thorough of US programme studies. It confirms that *Work First* approaches tend to work better than human capital development approaches, which give relatively greater scope to participation in training or education programmes. *Work First* approaches help more benefit claimants leave the welfare rolls and also help programme participants to achieve higher earnings than human capital development programmes do. This said, few US human capital development programmes for welfare recipients offered substantial training or education as part of their activities, and most were of short duration. Impacts from such programmes would, hence, be expected to be small.

The research findings also suggest that higher levels of programme sanctioning rates result in larger effects on earnings and larger reductions in the receipt of AFDC (Chapter 6). They also imply that if a programme can increase the number of participants who engage in job search, it will, as a result, have larger effects. On the other hand, increases in participation in basic or remedial education, vocational training, or work experience do not appear to result in larger increases in earnings or, and with the exception of vocational training, larger reductions in the AFDC rolls.

All these findings, but for the one concerning the relation between vocational training and the size of the AFDC rolls, are consistent with the superiority of the work-first approach over an approach that emphasizes human capital development. Moreover, when welfare-to-work programmes were categorized as having either a work-first or a human capital approach, the earnings effects of programmes in the former category lasted about as long as those for programmes in the latter category, but were much larger throughout most of the time they existed. Thus, the additional earnings attributable to the work-first approach appear far greater than those resulting from the human capital approach.

Some recently evaluated welfare-to-work programmes not only provided job search and training services, but also limited the length of time that families may remain on the AFDC rolls and incorporated incentives that financially reward programme participants who take jobs. Findings from the meta-analysis imply that inclusion of financial incentives in a welfare-to-work programme substantially reduces its effect on the receipt of AFDC, probably by raising the earnings disregard and thereby increasing the amount of earnings that recipients can receive, yet remain on the AFDC rolls. However, contrary to intensions, financial incentives do not appear to increase earnings. As expected, the imposition of time limits on the receipt of AFDC appears to have accelerated the process of leaving AFDC rolls, even though few programme participants had actually reached the time limit during the evaluations of any of the programmes in our sample that had this provision.

Additional findings from the meta-analysis indicate that effects are greater for programmes with a larger or predominantly white caseload than for programmes with mainly non-white participants, for persons who did not work during the year prior to random assignment than for those who did, and for older participants than for younger participants. They also appear to be larger when labour markets are tighter (that is, when unemployment rates are relatively low) and in states with less generous AFDC payment levels. Thus, it is important to stress that the characteristics of programme target population and socio-economic conditions at the programme sites can be as important as the characteristics of the programme that is run.

Special Cases: Riverside and Portland

A special effort was made in the meta-analysis to examine Riverside's and Portland's welfare-to-work programmes, as they have often been held up as models that are worthy of emulation. The prominence of these two programmes is due to the fact that well-conducted random assignment evaluations of them indicated that they were exceptionally effective. As described in Chapter 6, we used meta-analytic techniques to investigate why these programmes produced more positive effects than most other such programmes in terms of increasing the earning of programme participants and decreasing dependence on AFDC. The meta-analysis provides several interesting insights.

It demonstrates, for example, that the strong showing of the welfare-to-work programmes in Riverside and Portland was due, in part, to certain features of their design. Among these features is the strong emphasis that both programmes placed on job search, Portland's heavy use of sanctions, and Riverside's lack of use of vocational training. Interestingly, these are all attributes usually associated with the work-first approach, although, as discussed in Chapter 6, the programmes run in Riverside and (especially) Portland did not slavishly follow the work-first model.

The findings also suggest, however, that the apparent superior performance of the Riverside and Portland programmes was only partly attributable to the design of these programmes and, hence, only partially due to factors under the control of those administering these programmes. Part is also attributable to certain contextual factors – for example, their somewhat older and mostly white caseloads. This insight is important because it suggests that other sites that attempt to replicate the Riverside or Portland programme models are unlikely to obtain identical effects if their contextual characteristics differ.

Summary

At a general level, the findings from the meta-analysis described in this book suggest that welfare-to-work programmes work best where they employ work-first approaches that focus on job search activities and resort to sanctioning and impose time limits. At a more specific level, this conclusion may oversimplify the case for welfare-to-work programmes.

First, the effectiveness of programmes is not just a matter of programme design and implementation, but is also influenced by the characteristics of programme participants and socio-economic conditions. The importance of these factors and their variability across programmes and programme sites call for flexible approaches to programme development. Supporting measures may be put into place to help programmes overcome obstacles posed by the racial, gender, or age composition of their participants. This might involve additional actors and agencies, or might be achieved through programme providers.

Secondly, socio-economic variations call for different area-based approaches. In relatively advantaged areas, programmes may want to target resources on particularly disadvantaged individuals or neighbourhoods. Conversely, in areas with few advantageous socio-economic characteristics or high unemployment, broad coverage may be preferable to specific targeting to ensure that programme activities reach deeply into these communities.

Thirdly, the analysis indicates that it is a combination of factors that determine the success or failure of welfare-to-work programmes. As noted above, the programme tested in Riverside California enjoyed exceptional success. However, this programme succeeded both because *and* despite of its mix of services and sanctions and the social and economic circumstances, in which it operated. Sanctions, to give but one example, may thus be a 'supportive' but not a 'necessary' component of welfare-to-work programmes.

To conclude, the search for a best-practice model of welfare-to-work has only just begun. The meta-evaluation showed that more recent welfare-to-work programmes appear to have been more successful in moving participants off AFDC than earlier interventions but no better at increasing earnings. To date, then, policy learning has at best been partial. What meta-evaluation offers is the prospect of systematic and cumulative advance in policy knowledge. However, while this research makes a useful contribution to understanding the effectiveness of US welfare-to-work programmes, further study of different impact measures and of policy processes and other contextual influences is also needed.

Challenges to Future Meta-Evaluations

Meta-evaluation moves beyond an ideographic approach to policy learning, based on particular programme evaluations, to a nomothetic one concerned with the identification of general principles and, perhaps, theories or even laws. It allows the effects of differences in both programme design and implementation to be assessed and the consequences of varying local circumstances and environment to be established. None of this is possible in single programme evaluations. Thus, meta-evaluation changes the form of the evaluation question from the narrow: 'Does it work?' to the more useful: 'What works best, when and where it works best, and for whom?' (Walker, 2002). Meta-analysis is located firmly within the tradition pioneered by the Cochrane and Campbell collaborations that seek explanatory power from replication, accumulation of evidence, rigorous review and synthesis. Hence, it is unlikely to play well with those who reject 'pragmatism', in which choice of method is separated from epistemology and matched to specific research questions (Patton, 2002). Equally important, quantitative meta-evaluation has the potential to be far more than the simplistic parody suggested by some critics (Pawson, 2002a, 2002b).

However, the powerful insights that can be generated by meta-evaluation need to be set alongside methodological concerns. Relatively few high quality evaluations exist in most policy domains. The welfare-to-work programmes in the US were chosen explicitly because they are comparatively numerous, but the meta-evaluation presented above is still constrained by sample size. Moreover, while the database assembled for this study comprises a comprehensive set of evaluations using random assignment, it does not contain a random sample of all welfare-to-work programmes. Therefore, difficulties in generalizing the results to different settings and new policy experiments remain.

To some extent the problem of generalising was exacerbated by the decision to include only random assignment evaluations in the meta-analysis. However, most evaluations of US welfare-to-work programme have, in fact, been done by random assignment. Limiting our sample to only those based on random assignment had the advantage of imposing a quality threshold on the evaluations included. Moreover, reflecting the common methodology, meant that many of the variables and measures used by evaluators were similar in definition, form and function. The standardisation of variables was further aided by the fact that all but two of the evaluations in our sample were conducted by only three research organisations.

On the other hand, random assignment has been criticized on epistemological, methodological and technical grounds (Heckmann and Robb, 1985; Heckman and Smith, 1995; Walker et al., 2003). It certainly focuses attention on outcomes rather than process. Moreover, randomisation is difficult to implement and, while the organisations conducting the evaluations have excellent credentials, it is probable that standards rose over the period covered by the database possibly introducing a further element of bias.

More generally, however, a key challenge for meta-analysis and evaluation is to ensure consistency of definition and measurement. Furthermore, to date, analysts have struggled to find appropriate ways to account for differences in either the quality of research design or execution – weighting by standard errors mainly takes account of variations in sample size rather than differences in the quality of design and execution. Moreover, evaluation information based on qualitative methodologies probably cannot be embraced within the meta-evaluation rubric, although excluding them could well introduce systematic bias.

Including repeated observations drawn from the same evaluations in the regression analysis violates assumptions of independence, while inconsistent measures of variables between policy experiments exacerbate the usual problem of measurement error. While patently imperfect as a method, meta-evaluation forces the policy analyst to confront the violation of assumptions that remain implicit and unrecognized in the casual reviews of evidence that underpin most policy learning.

Although the obstacles to meta-evaluation are by no means trivial, some could be addressed comparatively easily by an evaluation community committed to cumulative policy learning and willing to adopt a long-term perspective. While not wanting overly to constrain evaluators, future meta-evaluation could be enhanced if certain practices were universally adopted. Based on our (admittedly) limited experience with conducting meta-analyses of welfare programme evaluations, we offer the following recommendations. Some have general applicability; others are specific to welfare programmes:

First, and most simply, reports of quantitative evaluations should provide exact standard errors or probability values (p-values) of programme effect estimates so that the weights needed for meta-analyses can be readily computed. When evaluation reports do not provide standard errors, it is necessary to impute them, possibly resulting in considerable error.

Second, if more than one programme effect is estimated in a given evaluation, the covariance structure of the estimates should be provided. This will enable meta-analysts to take these interdependencies into account when modelling the variation in programme effects.

Third, it is critical that studies not only provide information on the programme services offered to participants, but also on the services actually received. Variation in programme participation rates is likely to be important for explaining variation in the effects of different programmes. Moreover, because control groups also generally have access to some services, their receipt of these services should also be documented. This is often, but not always, done. Knowledge of the services available to control group members permits the meta-analyst to compute net rates of receipt of particular services for the experimental group being evaluated, which are more likely to explain variation in programme effects than gross rates of receipt.

In addition, better information about the intensity and, possibly, the content of education and training courses taken up by participants would also be helpful for improving our understanding of the effectiveness of welfare-to-work interventions. Whether a participant attended a three-day, four-week or a 3-month course, a full-time or a part-time course, and whether she was told about social and time-keeping skills, or was trained in literacy and numeracy rather than computing and typing skills might all influence the impact of programmes (see Fay, cited in Chapter 7). Similar information about the management of welfare-to-work programmes and the delivery of their services, as analysed by Bloom et al. (2001) and mentioned in Chapter 6, would also help improve our understanding of the various factors that affect the outcomes of these programmes and how these factors interact.

Fourth, moving slightly beyond the basic minimum expected of scientific reportage, more consistent reporting practices across evaluation studies would greatly facilitate meta-evaluation and synthesis in general. For example, it would be very helpful if all studies reported the same key population characteristics (the average age of the sample population, the percentage with a high school education, and so forth).

Finally, meta-evaluation would be greatly facilitated if different evaluations estimated programme effects for a similar set of subgroups. The importance of estimating programme effects for different subgroups is discussed in Manski (2001).

To conclude by moving from methodological detail to grand design, a quantitative meta-analysis is not the endpoint of evaluation but part of the ongoing process; the outcome is not the mean of means based on crass empiricism (Pawson, 2002a), but a better appreciation of the strengths and weaknesses of theory. Meta-analysis gains its power from its unique ability to test hypotheses about what is likely to work well or badly in different settings, and to develop new ones when old hypotheses are refuted. The stronger the prior theory, the stronger the method and the more secure the interpretation.

Just how universal such theory should be presumed to be is a moot point. The analysis embraced policy variants in 64 settings but it and the systematic review that preceded it were bounded by the US national border. Nevertheless, Chapter 3 maps the influence of US welfare-to-work policies on New Labour's New Deal programmes in the UK. This international trade in policy ideas would suggest that there might be a 'market' for cross-national meta-evaluation. However, the limitations of existing comparative policy analysis point to the conceptual and practical difficulties of achieving this (Walker and Such, forthcoming).

Policy Transfer and Learning – from the US to the UK

Evaluation methodology has experienced a process of rapid transformation and considerable advancement in the last two or so decades. Much of this methodological development originated in the United States and the exchange of ideas between the US and the UK in the area of welfare reform policy has – as we have shown in Chapters 2 and 3 – been intrinsically linked to this process of research innovation. But it has never been dependent upon it.

US evaluators have had notable and direct influence on the way in which evaluation research in the UK developed in the last ten or so years. However, it was the findings of their research, rather than the promotion of their methodological approach, that mainly shaped research and policymaking in the UK. The research findings themselves were of paramount importance, but, as argued in Chapter 2, it is impossible and would be misleading, if, in describing the processes of policy transfer and policy learning, personal connections, affiliations and preferences were not acknowledged.

These formal and informal linkages operate at two levels. At one level, the community of social researcher and policy analysts in the UK has, for some time, shared an interest and, indeed, a critical respect for the quality and the positivist-empiricist nature of US evaluation research. Personal contacts and projects of collaboration have consolidated such interests, helped by a shared language and a liberal cultural tradition, which, in turn, have facilitated many of the exchange visits between UK and US-based researchers and civil servants.

At another level, illustrated in a recent contribution by Daguerre (2004) and attested to by policymakers interviewed for this study, broad similarities between the UK and the US labour market, and a shared understanding of welfare principles, greatly facilitated collaboration and exchanges between the policy communities in the two countries. UK policymakers and analysts see the US as a vast arena for policy experimentation, which can yield insights for the development of policy in the UK. It cannot be said that the same perception exists among US policymakers and analysts, for whom there have always been less incentive and inclination to observe and monitor developments in policy making outside their own territory or regional territories. Especially among the policy-making community, interest and curiosity in welfare reform case studies tended to be greater in the UK than the US.

The Lessons that were Learned

As was seen in Chapter 2, UK policymakers and politicians actively sought information about welfare reform programmes internationally, travelling abroad to visit the sites of such programmes or to observe new approaches in labour market and welfare policy. These exploratory visits were not confined to the US, but also included Australia and New Zealand as frequent destinations. In most, if not all instances, learning about methods of activation was the principal rationale for these journeys. Although these excursions were about information gathering and learning, they never led to the wholesome adoption of any of the programmes and approaches that were observed. Policy transfer was partial and selective.

There was never a clear and deliberate strategy to inform and shape welfare reform policy in the UK through observations and enquiries abroad. Although some modalities of the New Deal were the result of discoveries away from home, such as the concept of the New Deal Gateway in Australia or the emphasis on work-first observed in the US, no product of welfare reform was ever wholesomely imported into the UK. Rather, policy observation resulted in an incremental process of policy learning, where pieces of information were collected and assembled together to form a new whole, which was to be called the New Deal.

It would probably have been impossible to import an activation model in its entirety or even the main components of such a model because, throughout its development, the New Deal remained deeply embedded in an inherited and, at the same time, evolving system of welfare policy-making and delivery. Moreover, padding out the New Deal and determining its components was a political, as well as a policy, process. As a result, the programme became a hybrid – built upon ideas and preferences, and concepts and experiences, emanating both at home and abroad. In fact, it would not be entirely inaccurate to describe the New Deal as an integrative framework that consists of a series of components, which had already existed independently prior to the programme. However, the New Deal is more than just that.

Policy Practice and Pragmatism

The integration of various policy initiatives as New Deal components enabled policymakers to accentuate some of these components more than others. As a by and large coherent and also comprehensive policy model, the New Deal has presented the framework, within which policymakers and politicians were able to firmly anchor their ideological concept of *rights and responsibilities*. From its inception, politicians, above all the Prime Minister and the Chancellor, promoted the New Deal as a programme without alternatives: there was to be 'no fifth option' beyond the four presented within the New Deal, especially the New Deal for Young People.

 The New Deal set new boundaries of choice, further narrowing the scope for non-participation in programmes by increasing the conditionality of benefit receipt, which the Labour Party had become to accept in its quest for political and electoral recognition. Within these boundaries, policy innovation and policy tradition met. Policy tradition meant that initiatives, which had been discredited as tools for labour market integration, such as voluntary work or the new Environmental Task Force, survived impending changes for very pragmatic reasons. For instance, publicly funded training, which because of its relative lack of success as a measure to help people into paid work had inspired many of the policy innovations and pilots of the 1990s, retained its place on the list of New Deal Options, albeit as a 'less favoured' option, as did voluntary work. At the same time, the inclusion of subsidized employment among the options was a concession to more cautious labour market economists, but only became financially feasible with the creation of the 'Windfall Tax'. All three became part of the New Deal in recognition of the fact that it might be difficult, if not impossible, to secure (unsubsidized) employment for all New Deal participants and that backup options, therefore, needed to be in place to maintain the programme's universal character.

 However, even these more traditional policies were embedded in new structures of policy delivery. The structures reflected the conviction, confirmed by emerging US welfare reform evidence, that direct and immediate job placements offered the surest and fasted route to reducing benefit caseloads. By emphasising the work-first principle, the New Deal explicitly acknowledged and accepted the lessons and messages emanating from the US. However, by inserting this principle in, and imposing it on top of a range of established policy options, the New Deal gave work-first a distinct British twist. The 13-week Gateway period of the New Deal provides an administrative, organisational as well as temporal distance between the (unsubsidized) work option and all other options, which accentuates the former. Yet, while firmly establishing the primacy of the work option, it leaves room for other, secondary activities, should the original objective of unsubsidized work not be achieved. The long-term nature of these secondary options sets the New Deal apart from any typical US welfare-to-work programme.

The integration of a traditionally more fragmented system of providing job training and placement for the unemployed was accompanied by one further innovation. Participants in previous labour market programmes primarily qualified on the basis of the duration of their unemployment or, in some cases, economic inactivity. The New Deal, in contrast, is targeted at specific 'sociological' client groups. Providing specialist programmes and services, and specialist advice to young people, the long-term unemployed, lone parents, disabled people, partners of the unemployed, or those aged 50 or over, the New Deal responds directly to the changing, diverse nature of joblessness. Although the New Deal has never operated as an overarching umbrella of service provisions, from which customized services for sociological groups with special needs could be extracted, its basic structure has nevertheless served as a conceptual framework, from which specialist programmes were developed.

Policy Learning *for* the New Deal

Learning from policy in the US – and indeed elsewhere – and importing ideas to the UK was always likely to have to compete with the realities of domestic policy-making. Nevertheless, important lessons were learned, and ideas and concepts absorbed into the New Deal programme. Conceptually, the key lessons that were learned from both the US and Australia were the means to translate an abstract concept, *rights and responsibilities,* into policy practice. This concept now characterizes current UK welfare policy.

The *right* to welfare was sustained through the almost *universal eligibility* for participation in the New Deal, which offers access to personal assistance to most categories of (long-term) unemployed or, indeed, some partners of the unemployed. It was also sustained through the offer of participation in the New Deal Options, including subsidized employment, which underlined the state's commitment to provide for a range of support needs. Importantly, however, the New Deal is not the only means used to address and alleviate unemployment and the associated high risk of poverty. The programme was always going to be flanked by legislation, for example, that introducing the National Minimum Wage and, more recently, Tax Credits designed to increase earnings or income and, in doing so, to enhance incentives and rewards for obtaining and maintaining paid work.

Responsibilities, on the other hand, are reflected in the *obligation* that requires most unemployed benefit claimants to participate in the New Deal or in a key component of the New Deal, the work-focussed interviews. This obligation has been subject to revisions. In the early years of the New Deal, participation was mandatory only for the long-term unemployed who were eligible for the New Deal for 25 plus, and for people aged 18 to 24 years, who were eligible for the New Deal for Young People. Since then, as noted earlier, lone parents, whose participation was initially voluntary, have been required to attend at least one meeting with a New Deal Personal Advisor, although they are still not required to agree to participation in any of the New Deal Options. The extension of mandatory participation of disabled people in initial work-focussed interviews with Personal Adviser is also being contemplated and is, in fact, currently being piloted outside the New Deal programme. Moreover, recent changes to the eligibility and claim rules of Jobseeker's Allowance, which require couples without anyone in work to make benefit claims jointly rather than individually, might yet strengthen the case for compulsory participation in the New Deal for Partners.

Modifications to the original New Deal programme were informed by evaluation and research evidence that pertained to the programme itself, rather than the findings of US evaluations. *Domestic* studies that highlighted the small, but positive effect of work-focussed interviews and of the New Gateway on New Deal participants' employment rates (e.g., Hales et al., 2000; Blundell et al., 2001), were particularly important.

For much of the 1990s, policymakers and policy analysts in the UK had only an incomplete and fragmented view of 'what works' in welfare-to-work. Evaluation evidence, in particular that emerging from the US, was often piecemeal, small-scale or based on case studies (see Chapters 3). Few US studies – and only one of the UK studies (White et al., 1997; see Chapter 7) – had a substantive comparative component, which could have produced a greater range and depth of insight into the working of welfare-to-work programmes in the UK and in the US. In the US, this is now changing, as more evaluations are being completed and published, and more of them are comparative (e.g. Hamilton, 2002). US welfare-to-work programmes, of course, are regionally diverse, but internally homogenous, as they typically target just one social group: lone parents. This increases the scope for comparative study. In contrast, the New Deal in the UK is a set of *national* programmes, which targets specific and (within each programme) uniform services at different social groups. This combination of characteristics limits opportunities for comparative impact assessments across New Deal programmes, although reviews of regional and local variations in the performance of programmes have been attempted (cp, NAO, 2002). However, descriptive comparisons of programmes other than the New Deal have been undertaken (Robinson, 2000; see also Chapter 7).

In the following sub-section, we consider whether the findings from the meta-analysis of US welfare-to-work programmes yield any important lessons for the UK New Deal.

Contrasting Lessons from Meta-Analysis

It cannot be claimed that findings from a meta-analysis of US welfare-to-work programmes would have immediate relevance to the UK New Deal, as the two sets of interventions operate in distinct social, economic and policy environments. This said, the US experience provides pointers as to *policy risks* that New Deal programmers already face or possibly should be prepared to face in the future.

Conclusion 1 – The client mix significantly affects programme impacts

The need to customize policy to meet the specific needs of individual client is embedded in the New Deal's separate provision of services of different social groups of unemployed or inactive people. The success of these separate programmes has varied, although it is as yet unclear as to whether this has been the result of variations in service provisions and their delivery, eligibility or obligation to participate, or the specificity of client needs and their propensity to enter employment.

The US evidence revealed that ethnic minorities, in particular black, Afro-Americans were significantly less likely to benefit from participation in welfare-to-work programmes, both in terms of reduced reliance on welfare payment and increased earnings, than white participants. A similar pattern has become apparent in the UK New Deal. Across most programmes, New Deal participants of ethnic minority background have been less successful in obtaining employment, be it through either direct placement or following their participation in one of the New Deal Options (TUC, 2004; see also Pettigrew, 2003). Policymakers are only beginning to address this issue.

Conclusion 2 – Environmental factors also influence the effectiveness of welfare-to-work programmes

The meta-analysis showed that, *ceteris paribus*, local unemployment and poverty rates have an independent effect on welfare-to-work programme impacts. The possibility that such factors could cause programme impacts to vary has never been explicitly acknowledged in the UK, although policy practice was soon alerted to the fact that the New Deal did not work equally well across the country (Turok and Webster, 1998). The New Deal is a national programme, and this restricts adaptation of programme features to match local conditions. Although the New Deal Innovation Fund offers opportunities to experiment at the local level and adjust provisions to meet specific needs, this does not yet amount to a concerted strategy of flexible delivery and provision.

The susceptibility of the New Deal to variations in external conditions is not limited to differences among locations, but also extends to changes over time. The New Deal's performance is unlikely to be unaffected by changes in economic conditions, nor will it escape the effects of social or political changes. Temporal change continues to be one of those policy risks that require further exploratory research, programme evaluation, and strategic reflection. If the long-term viability of the New Deal is to be secured, then unforeseen, adverse changes need to be kept to a minimum.

Conclusion 3 – Impacts are typically small, in particular the net earnings improvements of programme participants

The US programme meta-analysis clearly showed the limited impact that welfare-to-work programme have had in the US. Caseloads were typically reduced by less than two percentage points per quarter, while a typical programme increased the annual earnings of participants by less than $400 (in 2000 prices) over those of non-participants. It is not unusual for public policy interventions to have limited impact, although some programmes do stand out for their exceptional success (see Chapters 6 and 7).

More longitudinal data would be needed to analyse the earnings effects of the New Deal for participants in greater detail. However, it is already apparent that the National Minimum Wage (NMW), which was initially introduced in the UK on 1 April 1999 to increase incentive to work by widening the gap between benefit receipt and low-wage income, may come to play a more important role in increasing the earnings potential of disadvantaged workers than the New Deal. The NMW is increased every year and recent rises have been above inflation levels. Thus, an increasing proportion of people on low wages should benefit from it over time.

Conclusion 4 – Impacts wear off

Impacts of welfare-to-work programmes in the US do not last forever. Earnings impacts typically peaked at around three years, but then declined and disappeared altogether after two or three additional years. Many people on low earnings may find it hard to progress unless they receive further assistance. Increasing earnings mobility, for instance, through the provision of in-work support to help those receiving low earnings improve their financial and occupational position, be it with their employer or through changing employers, is one way of providing such assistance (Kellard et al., 2002). In the UK, some New Deal and similar job search and placement programmes are beginning to provide in-work support services, although they are typically underused and insufficiently promoted. The UK Employment Retention and Advancement (ERA) experiment is a major, large-scale endeavour to provide and test in-work support measures systematically on a pilot basis (Morris et al., 2003).

Conclusion 5 – Programmes come at a cost

Finally, welfare-to-work programmes have a price. They incur service and staff costs, and through the provision of financial incentives to programme participants require direct expenditure. Although US and UK experience suggests that welfare-to-work programmes induce a net reduction in the cost of welfare, the provision of services remains costly and may yet increase with the growing complexity of service requirements (e.g. in-work support programmes). This is because the policy and political need for support programmes for the unemployed is unlikely to diminish.

Moreover, the introduction of some of the New Deal programmes, in particular the New Deal for Partners and the New Deal for Young People, has, like some of the recent UK tax credit reforms, widened the circle of those eligible for (or obligated to participate in) welfare reform programmes. By drawing more people into the 'welfare class' (Walker with Howard, 2000), the New Deal has increased the British welfare state's actual and potential caseload.

To-date, the New Deal has benefited from a nationally declining unemployment rate, which has also reduced the number of those eligible for programme participation and, fortuitously, helped to stabilize spending levels. As mentioned in Chapter 3, one policy analyst has remarked that one of the main features of the job-seeking requirement introduced with the Jobseeker's Act of 1996 and maintained by the New Deal is that it presented jobseekers with an obligation to a 'self-service', for which the public sector incurred relatively little cost. Against this, the exhaustion of the Windfall Tax fund and any increase in unemployment would place pressure on the government to finance an expanded New Deal that goes well beyond enforced active job seeking and includes more costly options, such as subsidized work.

A Way Forward with Meta-Analysis?

This book set out to explore the impacts of US welfare-to-work programmes, systematically taking account of available evaluation evidence by using meta-analysis. Although meta-analysis was found to be methodologically challenging in terms of the range of data required and the needed standardization of data, it also emerged as a versatile instrument suitable for critically reviewing and assessing the cumulative evidence of the effectiveness of public policy.

For the most part, our meta-analysis relied on evaluations, which had been published before, sometimes long before, the launch of the UK New Deal programme. Imagine for a moment that, the meta-analysis findings derived from our study, would have been available in 1997. Would the New Deal have looked any different? It should have! A more critical look at the social and economic contexts, in which welfare-to-work programmes are situated, a greater concern for detail in programme delivery and management and (perhaps) less public emphasis on the mandatory nature of participation, should have produced a better programme.

Some of these lessons, although by no means all, are now being learned and policies are being adjusted accordingly. But even when policy lessons, for example, those drawn from the meta-analysis and, more recently, from the practical experience of implementing the New Deal programmes and from evaluations of these programmes, are clear and well understood, policy change that result from these lessons have been slow in materialising. Perhaps, this might not have been the case had a systematic review of evaluation evidence been available earlier.

Learning from exceptional cases, most notably the Riverside and Portland, Oregon welfare-to-work programmes, while ignoring more typical programmes, risks drawing misleading conclusions. Only comparative study can yield a baseline, which helps to highlight and to understand why some interventions are sometimes more effective than others. Meta-analysis can provide the appropriate tool for such a study. But policymaking is also the art of compromise and opportunity. It would be wrong to expect too much from the tool of meta-analysis in terms of its ability to inform policy. Yet, if policy is to be informed by experience – and, after all, this is why government departments commission research and evaluations – policymakers need to adopt a long-term, comparative perspective. Meta-analysis that builds on an archive of information has the potential to be at the methodological core of policy analysis by serving as an important tool for extracting knowledge that policymakers need by drawing upon both achievements and failures. Moreover, it has the capacity to update its knowledge base as new data become available.

References

Bloom, H., Hill, C. and Riccio, J. (2001), *Modelling the performance of welfare-to-work programmes: the effects of programme management, services, economic environment, and client characteristics*, MDRC, New York.

Blundell, R., Costa Dias, M., Meghir, C., and v. Reenan, J. (2001), *Evaluating the employment impact of a mandatory job search assistance programme*, Working Paper WP01/20, Institute for Fiscal Studies, London.

Daguerre, A. (2004), 'Importing Workfare: Policy Transfer of Social and Labour Market Policies from the USA to Britain under New Labour', *Social Policy and Administration*,Vol. 38.1, pp. 41-56 .

Fay, R.G. (1996), *Enhancing the effectiveness of active labour market policies: evidence from programme evaluations in OECD countries*, OECD Labour Market and Social Policy Occasional Papers No. 18, OECD, Paris.

Field, F. (1995), *Making Welfare Work: Reconstructing welfare for the Millennium*, Institute of Community Studies, London.

Greenberg, D., Michalopoulos, C. and Robins, P.K. (2003), A Meta-Analysis of Government Sponsored Training Programmes, *Industrial & Labor Relations Review*, vol. 57.1, pp. 31-53.

Hales, J., Lessof, C., Roth, W., Gloyer, M., Shaw, A., Millar, J., Barnes, M., Elias, P., Hasluck, C., McKnight, A., and Green, A. (2000) Evaluation of the New Deal for Lone Parents: Early Lessons from the Phase One Prototype, Synthesis Report, DSS Research Report 108, Corporate Document Services, Leeds.

Hamilton, G. (2002), *Moving People from Welfare to Work. Lessons from the National Evaluation of Welfare-to-Work Strategies*, MDRC, New York.

Heckman, J. and Robb, R. (1985), 'Alternative methods for evaluating the impact of interventions: An overview', *Journal of Econometrics*, vol. 30.1-2, pp. 239-267.

Heckman, J.J. and Smith, J.A. (1995) 'Assessing the Case for Social Experiments', *Journal of Economic Perspectives*, Vol. 9.2, pp. 85-100.

HM Treasury (1997), *The modernisation of Britain's tax and benefit system: Employment opportunity in a changing labour market*, Pre-Budget Publications, Number 1, HM Treasury, London.

HM Treasury (2000), *Tackling Poverty and Making Work Pay –Tax Credits for the 21st Century, The modernisation of Britain's tax and benefit system, Number 6*, HM Treasury, London.

Kellard, K., Adelman, L., Cebulla, A. and Heaver, C. (2002), *From Job Seekers to Job Keepers: Job Retention, Advancement and the Role of In-work Support Programmes*. Research Report No.170, Department for Work and Pensions, London.

Manski, C. (2001), 'Designing Programs for Heterogeneous Populations: The Value of Covariate Information', *American Economic Review*, vol. 91.2, pp. 103-106.

Morris, S., Greenberg, D., Riccio, J., Mittra, B., Green, H., Lissenburgh, S., and Blundell, R. (2003), *Designing a Demonstration Project. An Employment, Retention and Advancement Demonstration for Great Britain*, Cabinet Office, London.

NAO (2002), *The New Deal for Young People. Report by the Comptroller and Auditor General*, The Stationery Office, London.

Pawson, R. (2002a), 'Evidenced-based policy: In search of a method', *Evaluation*, vol. 8.2, pp. 157-181.

Pawson, R. (2002b), 'Evidence-based policy: The promise of 'realist synthesis'', *Evaluation*, vol. 8.3, pp. 340-358.

Pettigrew, N. (2003) *Experiences of lone parents from ethnic minority communities*, Research Report No. 187, Department for Work and Pensions, London.

TUC (2004), *The New Deal and Race*, TUC Welfare Reform Series No. 53. Trades Union Congress, London.

Robinson, P. (2000), 'Active labour-market policies: a case of evidence-based policy-making?', *Oxford Review of Economic Policy*, vol. 16.1, pp. 13-26.

Turok, I. and Webster, D. (1998), 'The New Deal: Jeopardised by the geography of unemployment?', *Local Economy*, vol. 12.4, pp. 309-328.

Walker, R. (2002), *Creating evaluative evidence for public policy*. Opening address to OECD conference on Evaluating Economic and Employment Development, Vienna, 20th November.

Walker, R. with Howard, M. (2000), *The making of the welfare class? Benefit receipt in Britain*, The Policy Press, Bristol.

Walker, R. and Such, E. (in preparation), *What is Comparative Social Policy?,*School of Sociology and Social Policy, University of Nottingham, Nottingham.

Walker, R., Greenberg, D., Ashworth, K and Cebulla, A (2003), 'Successful welfare-to-work programs: were Riverside and Portland really that good?', *Focus*, vol. 22.3, pp. 11-18.

White, M., Lissenburgh, S. and Bryson, A. (1997), *The Impact of Public Job Placing Programmes*, Policy Studies Institute, London.

Index